STAGGERING
LOVE

STAGGERING LOVE

Forging real relationships
in a fractured world

JOHN H. KIESCHNICK

A conversation about Paul's letter to the Ephesians

Cover design and interior formatting by Anne McLaughlin, Blue Lake Design, Dickinson, Texas

ISBN: 978-1-888237-91-7

Published by Baxter Press
Printed in the United States

Note: All the stories in this book are true, but in a few cases, names and details have been changed to protect anonymity.

This book is dedicated to seven congregations—different in so many ways but similar as manifestations of the body of Christ in the world...

. . . Zion Lutheran Church in Walburg, Texas, where I was baptized into the Christian faith when I was 10 days old and nurtured by loving parents, family, pastor, and teachers.

. . . Redeemer Lutheran Church in San Antonio, Texas, where I attended grades 5 through 8, and who supported me spiritually and financially while I attended prep school and junior college in Austin, Texas, senior college at Concordia Teachers College in River Forest, Illinois, and Concordia Theological Seminary in Springfield, Illinois.

. . . Calvary Lutheran Church, Havertown, Pennsylvania, where I served as teacher, principal, youth director, and bus driver of their church and school and was loved deeply by the pastor and his family, as well as the members there who encouraged me to become a pastor.

. . . Jehovah Lutheran Church in Chicago, Illinois, where I served my vicarage year as part of my seminary training from 1968-69, and learned that an earlier immigrant church (i.e. German) could transition to care for people in their changing neighborhood.

. . . Our Redeemer Lutheran Church in Irving, Texas, where I cut my teeth in the pastoral ministry in a mission church whose people taught me as much as I taught them.

. . . Gloria Dei Lutheran Church in Houston (Nassau Bay), Texas, where God blessed me and my family beyond measure for 33 years as we all partnered together for the greatest cause in the world, the cause of Jesus Christ.

. . . Trinity Lutheran Church in Houston, Texas, where my family and I are now being spiritually fed in my "repositioned" years, learning what it means to listen from the other side of the pulpit.

In their own ways, each congregation has been an example of staggering love to me and my family. Therefore, with sincere thanks to God for his marvelous grace in and through them, I wholehearted dedicate this book to them.

CONTENTS

ACKNOWLEDGEMENTS

This is the second book I was certain I would never write! What was true the first time around is true the second time as well. I want to thank many individuals and groups who have contributed first to bless my life, and then to lead the production of this book. Thanks to . . .

My family, in which I experienced the staggering love of Christ in remarkable ways. The model of my godly parents and my eight brothers and sisters (and their extended families) astounds me. In this setting, I experienced the unconditional love of God in Christ in very tangible ways.

My wife, Elaine, and our three children, Jonathan, Kimberly, and Jason, who have shared the grace of God with me in some of life's best and worst of times. Together we have learned that God's grace is the ultimate glue that holds a family together.

The staff of Gloria Dei Lutheran Church who encouraged me to write my first book, and the leadership of Gloria Dei who were willing to take the risk to do so a second time. Without their encouragement and support, neither book would have ever been written. Thanks to Vince Parks, Gloria Lastinger, Michelle Gooding, and many other partners in the faith.

Pat Springle of Baxter Press, who has guided the production of this book from start to finish. Pat is not just a good friend, he is a brother in Christ to me, another visible evidence of God's grace to me. One of the most frequent comments I received after my first book was published was summarized in these words, "Pastor K, reading your book was like having you sit on a couch in our living room and talk with us." There was good reason for this comment. Pat recorded hours of our conversations together, poured over many pages of printed manuscripts I had written, and then he crafted the book accordingly. I am eternally grateful for Pat's willingness to cooperate with me in this exciting venture.

Finally, to St. Paul, who, inspired by the Holy Spirit, penned this letter to the Christians in Ephesus and thereby enriched not only their lives but my life and the lives of countless others!

"Grace be with you all who love our Lord Jesus Christ with love incorruptible" (Ephesians 6:24).

INTRODUCTION

THE BACKSTORY

By reading the scriptures I am so renewed that all nature seems

renewed around me and with me. The sky seems to be a pure, a

cooler blue, the trees a deeper green. The whole world is charged

with the glory of God and I feel fire and music under my feet.

—Thomas Merton

As Elaine and I stood amid the ruins of the great city of Ephesus, I could almost hear Paul's voice echo through the centuries. Over the years, I have been able to take two tours of the Holy Land and the Near East. Elaine accompanied me on the first trip, and my brother Mel and I led a tour on another occasion. We traveled to Jerusalem and much of Israel, and we walked the streets of ancient Athens, Philippi, Corinth, Thessaloniki, Perea, Troas, and other cities where Paul first shared the good news of Jesus Christ. Ephesus had been one of the greatest cities of the world, a major trade center on the western coast of Asia (now Turkey). The Temple of Diana was one of the Seven Wonders of the ancient world. The city's theater seated 25,000 people and was connected to the temple. The acoustics were so good that every person could hear the actors on the theater platform. As we followed our tour guide, we gazed up at massive marble columns, and we looked down at intricate, colorful mosaics in the floors of the houses of the wealthiest citizens. Ephesus was a bustling port, a crossroads of east and west. People could get anything they wanted there. Our guide told us signs had been posted to direct sailors to brothels near the docks. It was New York and Las Vegas rolled into one.

Several centuries later, the city was abandoned because the river filled with silt and was no longer navigable, earthquakes ravaged the area, and outbreaks of malaria devastated the population. At the time Paul walked these streets, however, Ephesus was at the zenith of its grandeur, influence, and beauty. If he wanted to have an impact for Christ on the Roman world, Paul needed to go to the centers of culture, commerce, and power. Ephesus was one of those cities. It was the scene of some of the most dramatic moments in the apostle's life.

Paul arrived in Ephesus after taking a long, circuitous route. He began his second missionary journey in the Syrian port of Antioch. The church commended him and his companion Silas "to the grace of the Lord" (Acts 15:40), and the two men began a trek to visit cities where Paul had preached the gospel on his first trip. They traveled to Paul's hometown of Tarsus, then to Derbe, Lystra, and Iconium. They then traveled to the far northwestern coastal city of Troas. There, God spoke to Paul in a vision, telling him to cross the sea into Europe for the first time. The two men were arrested in Philippi for casting a demon out of a girl, but they were miraculously freed when God caused an earthquake that shook their chains off. The jailor was duly impressed. He and his family trusted in Christ and were baptized that very night.

Paul and Silas continued their tour of Greece, traveling to Berea, Thessalonica (now known as Thessaloniki), Athens, and Corinth. They then sailed across the Adriatic Sea to Ephesus. On this trip, they stayed only a short time, but he promised them, "I will return to you if God wills" (Acts 18:19-21).

It didn't take Paul long to make good on his promise. After a short stay in Antioch to give his report of how God was working in distant lands, Paul made the overland trip back to Ephesus. He preached in the synagogue, but when some Jews resisted him, he moved his followers to a new site and taught them in the hall of Tyrannus. In all, Paul stayed in Ephesus longer than any other city where he traveled. Many scholars believe he invested three years in the lives of the people there. Of course, he wasn't content to have a localized impact. Luke tells us, "All the residents of Asia heard the word of the Lord, both Jews and Greeks" (Acts 19:10).

While Paul was in the city, two important events occurred. When Luke described the first one, I can imagine him having a bit of a smirk on his face. God used Paul to perform many miracles. In fact, people took handkerchiefs and aprons from him to heal the sick and free those who were demon-possessed. At one point, some traveling exorcists were impressed with God's power displayed through Paul. The seven sons of a priest named Sceva began to talk to the demons by saying, "I adjure you by the Jesus whom Paul proclaims." The demon realized these men were only mimicking Paul's spiritual authority. The man possessed by the demon "leaped on them, mastered all of them and overpowered them, so that they fled out of that house naked and wounded" (Acts 19:16). Everybody in the city heard this story, and they were amazed by the power (and humor) of God.

The second significant event caused a broader social and economic explosion. So many people in Ephesus were coming to Christ that the market for silver idols collapsed. A silversmith named Demetrius gathered his guild and complained, "There is danger not only that this trade of ours may come into disrepute but also that the temple of the great goddess Artemis may be counted as nothing, and that she may even be deposed from her magnificence, she whom all Asia and the world worship" (Acts 19:27). Demetrius had hit the bull's eye on the economic problem created by the impact of the gospel. He and the others started a riot against the Christians. Soon, both sides stormed into the theater to plead their case. Paul wanted to jump into the middle of it, but his disciples stopped him. For two hours, the angry crowds shouted at each other. Finally, the town clerk stepped forward and quieted them.

The riot was at the end of Paul's long stay in Ephesus during his second journey. On his third missionary journey, he traveled from city to city through the regions of Galatia and Phrygia strengthening the disciples. He traveled to Macedonia and then to Greece. He retraced some of his steps on his way back to Jerusalem for the feast of Pentecost. He came to Miletus, a town a few miles south of Ephesus. He sent for the Ephesian elders, and they came to meet him. He wanted to give them one last word of warning and encouragement. He predicted they would encounter difficulties in the culture and in the church, and he gave them an impassioned, honest plea to remain true to Christ. He told them,

> "And now, behold, I am going to Jerusalem, constrained by the Spirit, not knowing what will happen to me there, except that the Holy Spirit testifies to me in every city that imprisonment and afflictions await me. But I do not account my life of any value nor as precious to myself, if only I may finish my course and the ministry that I received from the Lord Jesus, to testify to the gospel of the grace of God" (Acts 20:22-24).

We often think of Paul as a tough guy, but as he closed his meeting with these men he loved, he reminded them to help the weak and be generous to the poor. He quoted Jesus: "It is more blessed to give than to receive." When he told them they would probably never see him again, they wept, embraced, and kissed him. There is no scene in Luke's account of the early church that shows as much tenderness, strength, tenacity, and commitment among followers of Jesus Christ.

When Paul arrived in Jerusalem, he was almost immediately arrested. The Jewish leaders wanted to kill him, but the Roman rulers kept him locked away in Caesarea. After a series of hearings, he appealed to the Roman Emperor and was shipped off to Rome. Under house arrest in the capital of the empire, Paul wrote a letter to the Christians in Ephesus. It was probably a circular letter intended to be read in every church in the region. The hallmarks of Paul's tender heart and clear message are found in every line. He penned the letter about five years after he parted from the elders in his last meeting with them.

Paul wrote to remind them of everything he had taught them during the nearly three years he lived in Ephesus. He wanted to reinforce the magnificent message of the grace of God in transforming lives. In this letter, Paul doesn't address problems in believers' beliefs and relationships (like the letters to the Corinthians) or doctrinal heresies (such as the letter to the Colossians). Paul understood it's human nature to drift away from the grace of God and the power of the Spirit. If we're not careful, we default to following rules to prove our worthiness, and we feel superior to those who don't follow them as well as we do. The purity and power of God's magnificent grace shatters those misconceptions, but we need to hear it again and again. Human nature hasn't changed in all these millennia. We still struggle with temptation, misplaced desires, blatant selfishness, and the tendency to drift away from the strong anchor of faith in God. People haven't changed, but neither has the grace of God.

Three years of good teaching wasn't enough for the people of Ephesus, and it's not enough for us, either. We need constant reminders of the wonders of God's incredible love, forgiveness, and acceptance found in Jesus Christ. Paul tells them (and us) that God's plan to rescue people from eternal darkness wasn't dreamed up yesterday. His purpose for us today and tomorrow was planned before the foundations of the world.

MY HOPE FOR YOU

Over the years, God has used Paul's letter to the Ephesians to inspire and challenge me. At times when I've felt discouraged, the truths of my identity as God's beloved child and his purposes for my life have instilled my heart with new hope. When I've wondered how the Christian life is meant to work, this letter has given me insights on the choices I make each day—as well as my motives for making them. There may not be another part of God's word that has had such a powerful and positive impact on my life.

You may be new to the faith and reading Paul's letter for the first time, or you may have studied it dozens of times over many years. No matter how you come to this study, I hope God opens the eyes of your heart so that you are astounded by the wonder of his greatness and grace. If we aren't amazed, it's not really grace we're looking at. When we get even a glimpse of Christ's heart for us, something wonderful happens: We're melted by his love, and his Spirit gives us strength to meet every challenge. Only God's grace can do both of those things.

As I pray for God to use this study in your life, I can't improve on Paul's prayer for the Ephesians. He prays that . . .

> . . . according to the riches of his glory he may grant you
> to be strengthened with power through his Spirit in your

inner being, so that Christ may dwell in your hearts through faith—that you, being rooted and grounded in love, may have strength to comprehend with all the saints what is the breadth and length and height and depth, and to know the love of Christ that surpasses knowledge, that you may be filled with all the fullness of God (Ephesians 3:16-19).

Love transforms our motivations. When our hearts are captured by Christ's love, we're freed from guilt and shame, and we want to imitate the one who proved his love by paying the ultimate price to call us his own.

The Christian life isn't just a set of rules to follow—it's a relationship with the God of the universe, who stepped out of the glories of heaven to rescue us from sin and death. God's plan, though, isn't just to save us so we can go to heaven when we die. He wants us to love him so much that we put ourselves in his hands so he can make us more like Jesus—now, today, in our present relationships and circumstances. When we grasp his grace, we "walk in love, as Christ loved us and gave himself up for us, a fragrant offering and sacrifice to God" (Ephesians 5:2). The experience of God's grace turns our "have to" into "want to." We don't remain spiritual infants. We grow "to the measure of the stature of the fullness of Christ" (Ephesians 4:13). We become more mature in our sense of identity, our purpose in life, all our relationships, choices, and responses to difficulties.

It's not enough to sit in church every week, and it's not enough to know right doctrines. Those are important, but God wants more for us—much more. He is reaching out to make us the incredible offer of a real relationship. When we take his hand, he lets us in on his magnificent purposes for our lives, our families, our work, our church, and our world. Paul's letter addresses the full range of human desires, needs, hopes, and fears. His answer is always rooted in the marvelous grace of Jesus, who forgives, restores, and propels us to accomplish more than we ever dared dream before.

In *Mere Christianity*, C. S. Lewis described God's purposes and processes:

> Imagine yourself as a living house. God comes in to rebuild that house. At first, perhaps, you can understand what He is doing. He is getting the drains right and stopping the leaks in the roof and so on; you knew that those jobs needed doing and so you are not surprised. But presently He starts knocking the house about in a way that hurts abominably and does not seem to make any sense. What on earth is He up to? The explanation is that He is building quite a different house from the one you thought of—throwing out a new wing here, putting on an extra floor there, running up towers, making courtyards. You thought you were being made into a decent little cottage: but He is building a palace. He intends to come and live in it Himself.[1]

Have you welcomed Christ in so he can build a palace? Are you ready to have your world turned upside down—in a good way? That's what God wants to do in your life and mine. So . . . let the reconstruction continue!

---

1   C. S. Lewis, *Mere Christianity* (HarperCollins: New York, 1952), p. 205.

1

EXTREME MAKEOVER

Ephesians 1:1-23

Real Christians are marked by sincerity—the whole truth about

themselves and the whole truth about God. Real Christians stand

before people the way they stand before God—transparent and

vulnerable. Anything less is a dressed-up Gospel.

—John Fischer

Every person on the planet is affected by radical insecurity. Some of us grew up in unstable homes, some have suffered traumatic losses, and others live under the crushing weight of chronic stress. It's easy to see how people like these feel insecure, but no one is exempt. The rest of humanity tries hard every day to cover up and compensate for the nagging sense that something's terribly wrong and they don't measure up.

We strive for positions so we'll feel important, but a month after we reach a new plateau, we feel just as empty. We long for intimacy and companionship, but we have a hard time finding someone we can trust with our deepest desires and fears. We wear masks of competence, politeness, or coolness to keep people away so they won't know what's really going on inside us. Radical insecurity isn't the exclusive province of those who are abused or abandoned. If we're honest, all of us have to admit we struggle with it. Insecurity is endemic to the human condition. We were made for more. We know it, but we can't figure out how to fill the hole in our hearts with possessions, titles, pleasures, and popularity. Those pursuits make promises they simply can't fulfill.

I know. I have my share of insecurities. I've always struggled with not feeling good enough, smart enough, or sharp enough. But my insecurity skyrocketed when an important relationship blew up and rocked my world. I had been a pastor for a while. Maybe I should have seen it coming, but it was still a stunning series of events. In case you think pastors and church leaders are somehow too godly to experience resentment and hurt, think again. If we're human, it can happen to any of us.

Perhaps I was choosing to ignore the obvious, but I must admit that I was completely caught off-guard. Our head elder asked to meet with me and the chairman of our board. I wondered why the chairman was invited to the meeting. I soon found out. From the moment we sat down, the elder launched into a litany of complaints about me and everything about my leadership—accusations he said had been shared with him by staff members. For almost an hour, he listed grievances. The look on his face told me he wasn't looking for resolution. I sensed he was out for blood! I felt like I was standing in front of a machine gun. From time to time, I looked over at the chairman of our board. I considered him a friend, but he just sat there listening and watching. I interpreted his demeanor as support for my accuser's rapid-fire list of allegations, although I learned later I had misread him.

Finally, the gun's magazine was empty. The elder sat back in his chair with a look of satisfaction. He leaned forward and asked, "John, tell me how you feel about all this."

I tried to compose myself, but it was very hard. I said slowly and deliberately, "I'll tell you how I feel. I feel like someone has dropped a load of crap on me."

The elder instantly tried to reframe the message that had been abundantly clear for almost an hour. He blurted out, "Oh, that's not how I hoped you'd respond at all! We were trying to help!"

If he was trying to help, he wasn't very convincing. All I could think to say was: "I'll tell you in 24 hours if I'm going to remain the pastor of this church."

When I got home and walked through the door, my body language must have screamed my inner thoughts and feelings. Elaine took one look at me and asked, "What in the world is wrong with you?"

I tried to avoid the conversation by saying, "Nothing."

She wasn't buying it. She insisted, "Don't tell me that. You're as pale as a ghost. Tell me what happened."

I told her about the conversation, and we asked God for wisdom. I questioned God's calling and purpose for my life—as the pastor of that church, and even as a pastor at all. Over the next day, I became deeply convinced that God had called me to that church and those people, so I agreed to stay. Still, I felt devastated. The encounter shattered my confidence as a leader and drove me into depression for several years. Yes, several years. I wish I could tell you I was immediately healed of my hurt, but I wasn't. God took me through the darkest days of my life and ministry to show me new aspects of his love and light. Much of what he showed me was that my sense of security had been in the wrong place.

After I told the church leadership I was going to stay, I asked three leading laymen in our church to be my confidantes and hold me accountable. I was terrified to be vulnerable with these men, but I knew it was the only way forward. I thought, *If they really know who I am— the mistakes, secrets, hopes, and fears—they'll laugh at me, run away from me, or ridicule me.* I knew honesty was a risk, but it was one I was willing to take. During this time, I also saw a member of the clergy who helped me see hidden hurts and patterns of responses that had been part of my life for years. So, in spite of the pain and misunderstanding of the confrontation, God was going to use it for good in my life.

During this difficult but revealing time, I came face to face with my dark side. I realized all of us have secret hopes and fears, and they can poison every aspect of our lives. Author and pastor John Ortberg says that our "shadow mission" often looks completely good and right, but it's insidious: "Our shadow mission leads us just five or ten degrees off our true path in the direction of selfishness or comfort or arrogance. But those few degrees, over time, become the difference between light and shadow."[2] We give, but to impress people. We serve, but to have power over others. We smile, but to hide the hurt we're unwilling to admit to anyone, even ourselves.

We don't overcome the darkness in our hearts on our own. God gives us wise, loving people to speak grace and truth into our lives. After I'd been meeting with these three men for several years, I preached on a Sunday morning but felt my message had fallen flat. I saw one of these men after the service and said, "Gary, I feel like a failure. I'm really struggling with my dark side."

He gave me a hug and said, "John, so am I. I love you. We'll go through this together." It was only a few seconds of interaction, but Gary's warmth and understanding meant the world to me. I had been vulnerable with him, and he had affirmed me deeply. It was one of the most redeeming moments of my life. Gary loved me even knowing the worst about me. That day, he was "God's grace with skin on" for me.

In the opening of Paul's letter to the Ephesians, he addresses the radical insecurities, secrets, and fears of every human heart. He begins by identifying himself and extends a greeting to his readers:

---

2   John Ortberg, *Overcoming Your Shadow Mission* (Zondervan: Grand Rapids, 2008), p. 36.

Paul, an apostle of Christ Jesus by the will of God,

To the saints who are in Ephesus, and are faithful in

Christ Jesus:

Grace to you and peace from God our Father and the Lord

Jesus Christ (1:1-2).

People need more than "happy talk" from their spiritual leaders. They long to know that God's love reaches into the deepest, darkest recesses of their souls where they've buried (or tried to bury) the sins, pain, and bitterness from the past. When I've talked about the reality of my own struggles in sermons, people often have come up to me to tell me how much my honesty has meant to them. They came to church that day hoping something or someone would be safe and reach into their hearts with authentic love, and they found honesty and authenticity. I know what it means to them because I know what it means to me. No matter how much success we enjoy, God is far higher and greater. And no matter how low we feel, God's grace is always deeper and wider. His grace humbles us and thrills us. With that assurance, Paul begins his letter.

FOUR PILLARS OF SECURITY

In his letters to the churches, Paul often makes a sweeping statement and then spends a lot of time unpacking it. In this letter, he wrote,

Blessed be the God and Father of our Lord Jesus Christ, who has blessed us in Christ with every spiritual blessing in the heavenly places (1:3).

The spiritual blessings Paul defines and describes are that God has *chosen* us, *adopted* us, *forgiven* us, and *sealed* us by his Spirit. These four concepts are the pillars that support our faith, our security, and our hope. Notice these concepts and the extravagant language Paul uses to describe them:

> . . . even as he chose us in him before the foundation of the world, that we should be holy and blameless before him. In love he predestined us for adoption as sons through Jesus Christ, according to the purpose of his will, to the praise of his glorious grace, with which he has blessed us in the Beloved. In him we have redemption through his blood, the forgiveness of our trespasses, according to the riches of his grace, which he lavished upon us, in all wisdom and insight making known to us the mystery of his will, according to his purpose, which he set forth in Christ as a plan for the fullness of time, to unite all things in him, things in heaven and things on earth.
>
> In him we have obtained an inheritance, having been predestined according to the purpose of him who works all things according to the counsel of his will, so that we who were the first to hope in Christ might be to the praise of his glory. In him you also, when you heard the word of truth, the gospel of your salvation, and believed in him, were sealed with the promised Holy Spirit, who is the guarantee of our inheritance until we acquire possession of it, to the praise of his glory (1:4-14).

Let's look at each of these pillars.

Chosen

Some people get all tied up in knots about the issue of predestination and free will. In our western minds, we want to make it *either/or*, but God is big enough to make it *both/and*. Author Philip Yancey quotes G. K. Chesterton and comments on Chesterton's insight: "In a memorable phrase that became the virtual cornerstone of his theology, G. K. Chesterton said, 'Christianity got over the difficulty of combining furious opposites, by keeping them both, and keeping them both furious.' Most heresies come from espousing one opposite at the expense of the other."[3] Paul certainly isn't trying to be controversial at the outset of his letter. Good writers don't do that! Instead, he wants to give the fullest assurance of God's love. The truth of God's sovereign choosing is the bedrock of our faith's security and certainty.

Do you remember what it was like when kids chose teams at recess when you were in grade school? Each person nervously waited . . . and some of us wondered if and when we'd ever get picked. When someone chooses us—for a kickball team, as a spouse, or for a promotion—it feels great! It's a thrill and a relief. We know we're valued, especially if the person picking us is highly respected. Now, Paul tells us that the God of the Universe, the great I Am, the one who spoke and flung billions of galaxies into space, looked to the speck of dust called earth and picked you and me to be his own. We weren't smart enough to pick him, and we weren't good enough to earn the position by our merit. He chose us to be his by his grace—*in spite of* our sins, darkness, fears, selfishness, and shadow desires.

The idea of God choosing us is as old as mankind. God reached into a hopeless family in a hopeless land to call Abraham to begin

---

3   Philip Yancey, *Reaching for the Invisible God* (Zondervan: Grand Rapids, 2000), p. 92.

a new kingdom of God. Through Isaiah, God assured his doubting, fear-plagued people, "Can a woman forget her nursing child, that she should have no compassion on the son of her womb? Even these may forget, yet I will not forget you. Behold, I have engraved you on the palms of my hands" (Isaiah 49:15-16). On the night before he was betrayed, Jesus told his disciples, "You did not choose me, but I chose you and appointed you that you should go and bear fruit and that your fruit should abide" (John 15:16).

I don't believe the doctrines of God's sovereign choice and our predestination are meant to provoke fierce theological debates or psychological fears. They certainly aren't a license to sin all we want. Paul's first blessing is God's loving act to pick each person who would become his own. His love becomes our motive to honor him in everything we do—to want to be "holy and blameless," not to prove our worth, but because we want to please the one who loves us so much. If we truly believe God has chosen us, many of our fears melt away in the solid assurance of his love, presence, and purpose.

Our assurance of salvation isn't based on how many times we go to church, whether we still cuss, how much money we give, or any other checklist of dos and don'ts. The anchor of our faith is God's divine right to choose us in Jesus Christ. We didn't contribute anything to his decision, so we can't take anything away from it. We are totally secure because of his grace, not because we've earned enough points with him.

Adopted

God could have chosen us to be his slaves, but he chose us to be his children. When parents adopt a child today, there is a moment when the legal documents are signed and the child becomes part of the new family. The transfer of identity is complete at that moment, but it often takes years for the adopted child to comprehend and experience the security and love of the new parents. In the same way, some of us wrestle with our adoption into God's family. We may have been abused or abandoned, so we find it hard to believe a new parent—even the perfect Father—truly loves us.

Adoption is one of the wonders of our faith. We often talk about God forgiving us for our sins and setting us free. Justification is, in fact, the solid foundation of faith, but adoption is an equally magnificent truth about our salvation. It's a relief when a judge declares us not guilty, but it's a marvel when a father claims us and takes us home.

When we read the New Testament, we see terms like "in Christ" and "in him." In our baptism, our new identity is inextricably and completely united with Christ. We've died with him, and we were raised in him. In his seminal book, *Knowing God*, author and professor J. I. Packer describes the wonder of this connection:

God . . . loves us with the same steadfast affection with which He eternally loves His beloved only-begotten. There are no distinctions of affection in the divine family. We are all loved just as fully as Jesus is loved. It is like a fairy story—the reigning monarch adopts waifs and strays to make princes of them— but praise God, it is not a fairy story: it is hard and solid fact, founded on the bedrock of free and sovereign grace. This, and nothing less than this, is what adoption means. No wonder that John cries, "Behold, what manner of love . . . !" When once you understand adoption, your heart will cry the same.[4]

Even the slightest grasp of the wonder of adoption causes our hearts to sing. We can't stop praising "his glorious grace."

---

4   J. I. Packer, *Knowing God* (InterVarsity Press: Downers Grove, 1973), p. 196.

Some women might read this passage and feel upset that Paul said God adopts us "as sons." They don't need to get upset. Instead, they can feel honored. Paul is turning conventional wisdom of the first century on its head! In that day, women were little more than property, but Paul says that every believer—Jew or Greek, male or female, slave or free—is *equally accepted* by God as his beloved children. We can imagine the thrill in the room among Greeks, women, and slaves as they heard someone read this letter! In God's family, everyone receives equal honor.

Forgiven

Another foundational blessing in the Christian life is forgiveness. Then as today, many misunderstood this concept. Forgiveness isn't excusing an offense ("It didn't really hurt me"), minimizing the wound ("It wasn't that bad"), or denying it ("What offense? I didn't notice anything wrong"). It looks evil right in the eye, calls it what it is, and chooses to absorb the debt incurred. Every sin costs the victim. When we sin against a spouse or friend, we create a hurt to be healed, a hole to be filled, a debt to be paid. When we sinned against God, it took a divine man living a perfect life and dying a sacrificial death to pay the price. Only one person fit that description: Jesus stepped out of heaven to bear the sins of the world as he died on the cross. In this letter, Paul says we have "redemption," a payment made for us. The price was "his blood." This is Pauline shorthand for Christ's death on the cross— foretold by the prophets, dreaded in the Garden of Gethsemane, and paid in full by Jesus' torture and death.

Jesus didn't dab his forgiveness on us. He poured it out "according to the riches of his grace, which he lavished upon us." Without this payment, we were hopeless and helpless. Grace isn't making pretty good people a little better—it's washing the filth from deeply flawed, filthy people who couldn't ever do enough to get clean by themselves.

We often say the basic human need is to love and be loved, but perhaps an even more basic need is to be forgiven. We don't come to God as empty vessels that need to be filled up with love. We come with "younger brother sins" of addiction, adultery, theft, and wild living, or we come with "elder brother sins" of bitterness, demands, and superiority. We desperately need to be forgiven. How does it begin? God has given us a conscience and the Holy Spirit to point out our sins. We often try to avoid feelings of guilt at all cost, but honestly facing our sin is the first step to experiencing the relief of God's forgiveness. In his book, , Philip Yancey wrote, "Guilt is the early warning sign of danger, the first rumor of something wrong."[5]

When I attended a pastors' conference years ago, the lead Lutheran chaplain at M. D. Anderson Cancer Center spoke to us. He asked, "What do you think terminally ill patients pray for most often?"

Several people instantly responded, "Healing."

He shook his head. "No, almost all of them pray for forgiveness." When all the trappings of life vanished from their crowded lives and their hearts became most sensitive to the Spirit, these people longed for God's cleansing grace. Luther wrote, "Where there is forgiveness of sins, there is life and salvation."[6]

I decided to test the chaplain and Luther. I asked a man who has suffered from polio for many years, "Ken, what do you pray for most often?"

He answered immediately, "To be forgiven, Pastor."

When we read the Scriptures and see where we fall short of God's law and demands, we have a choice. Like Adam in the garden, we

---

5   Philip Yancey, *Rumors of Another World*, (Zondervan: Grand Rapids, 2003), p. 145.
6   Martin Luther, cited by Robert Kolb and Charles P. Arand in *The Genius of Luther's Theology* (Baker Academic, 2008), p. 198.

can blame our spouse and God. We can try to hide our sins and hope no one notices, or we can attempt to do enough penance to make up for our faults, hoping that somehow our actions will balance the scales and let us off the hook. We often rationalize our sinful behavior. Some people say that the Greek word for sin in the Bible is an arrow "missing the mark." That may be true, but I've seen a lot of people (including the guy I see in the morning when I'm shaving) who shoot the arrow and then run to move the target so we don't miss it. We say we're not bitter—just frustrated. We're not selfish—we're just taking care of ourselves. We weren't rude—just speaking our minds. We weren't lying—we were telling a "better" story. Quite often, we look around at others and sneer, "Well, at least I'm not that bad!" Comparison may make us feel good for the moment, but it produces a sense of superiority that blocks the channel of God's love.

None of these strategies deals with the root issue of our sin and guilt. God's law isn't the enemy. It's God warning signal designed to get our attention so we'll turn to him in humility and faith. Only then can we experience the fullness of his great grace, the relief of forgiveness, and the motivation to live for his great purposes instead of our selfish desires.

Paul reminds us that God's grace and forgiveness have been his plan since time began. He didn't come up with it over a cup of coffee this morning. The "fullness of time" began when Jesus lived, died, and was raised from the dead, but its complete fulfillment won't occur until some time in the future. Today, we live between the "already" and the "not yet." We have a taste of God's presence and the assurance that God will use every event to accomplish his purposes, but someday in the new heaven and new earth, we'll walk with him arm in arm. On that day, every wrong will be made right, every tear turned to laughter, and God's light will shatter the darkness. On that day, God's chosen, adopted children will receive their full inheritance of riches, love, and purpose. If you think your grandmother's silver was a wonderful inheritance, you ain't seen nothing yet!

Sealed

In the Roman Empire, officials used seals on documents, doors, and boxes to signify security and ownership. When the soldiers wanted to make Jesus' tomb secure, they put a seal on it and placed a guard outside it. In his letter to the Ephesians, Paul uses this image to explain the Holy Spirit's role in our lives. When someone believes in Jesus, he is "sealed with the promised Holy Spirit." The Spirit accomplishes many different things for believers: Among others, he assures us that we're God's children, imparts special talents, places us in the body, causes spiritual growth, and increasingly produces the character of Christ in us. Our experience of the Spirit now, however, is only a taste of what's to come. Today, the Spirit's presence and power at work in our lives is "the guarantee of our inheritance until we acquire possession of it." Other translations say the Spirit is a down payment, deposit, or earnest, with the promise of far more to come in the new heaven and new earth.

This passage reminds us of the beautiful working of the Trinity. The Father chose us, the Son paid our debt, and the Spirit seals us for time and eternity. This reminds me of the statement made at our baptism. We're baptized "in the name of the Father, the Son, and the Holy Spirit." We don't relegate the importance of the Trinity to special occasions. Luther recommended that we get up every morning, make the sign of the cross, and remember that we've been baptized in the name of the Father, Son, and Holy Spirit. Then, fortified by the reminder of God's glory and grace, we go out into the world. A seminary professor posted his baptismal certificate on his back door so he would see it every day when he left the house. In the same way, when we go through the day, we can recall—in times of joy and times of stress—that at our baptism we entered a new relationship with God: We've been chosen, adopted, forgiven, and sealed. God planned to pour out his blessings on us before time began, and he pours them out in abundance. It's amazing grace . . . staggering love, but it's not over yet. The best is yet to come.

We don't need to be angry, afraid, or embarrassed about the biblical truth of predestination. If we understand it properly, it is one of the most inspiring concepts in our Bibles! It is taught to "reassure the conflicted sinner" of God's great love. It doesn't negate our ability to choose, but it means God chose first. He wanted us. He didn't need us, we don't deserve his love and mercy, but he chose us anyway. Don't miss this. It's one of the keys to understanding the nature of grace.

Do you doubt God's love? You can't earn it so you can't lose it.

Do you wonder if you've sinned so badly you're beyond hope? God's grace is far greater than all our sin.

Do you suffer from nagging guilt and fear? Be assured that God doesn't just tolerate you. He chose you and lavishes his love on you. He's delighted to have you as his child—not because you're good enough, but in spite of all your flaws and faults. That's the nature and measure of his grace.

GOD, OPEN MY HEART

After this magnificent opening statement about God's grace, love, and power, Paul breaks into prayer. He asks God to make the truths of the first paragraphs real in our experience. It's not enough just to know them as doctrine—we need to sense their life-changing power in the depths of our souls. Notice the connections between the truths he just taught and his petition to God:

> For this reason, because I have heard of your faith in the Lord Jesus and your love toward all the saints, I do not cease to give thanks for you, remembering you in my prayers, that the God of our Lord Jesus Christ, the Father of glory, may give you the Spirit of wisdom and of revelation in the knowledge of him, having the eyes of your hearts enlightened, that you may know what is the hope to which he has called you, what are the riches of his glorious inheritance in the saints, and what is the immeasurable greatness of his power toward us who believe, according to the working of his great might that he worked in Christ when he raised him from the dead and seated him at his right hand in the heavenly places, far above all rule and authority and power and dominion, and above every name that is named, not only in this age but also in the one to come. And he put all things under his feet and gave him as head over all things to the church, which is his body, the fullness of him who fills all in all (1:15–23).

How do people "get it"? What makes the lights come on in a person's heart so she's overwhelmed with the grace of God? Reading the Bible certainly contributes, and going to church and participating in the Lord's Supper remind us of God's truth, but we know plenty of people who have read and attended for years without experiencing a transformed heart—and some who fit this description may be reading this book.

When Jesus told his famous parable of the two brothers, commonly called "The Prodigal Son," the younger brother left home to spend his inheritance on a wild lifestyle. He blew it all and found himself destitute and alone, feeding pigs and eyeing the pig slop because he was so hungry. At that moment, he "came to his senses" and started for home. When a person is in a coma, he doesn't decide to wake up. It happens *to* him. In the same way, we don't wake up spiritually until and unless God does the work to awaken us. It's a work of God's grace to give us eyes to see. When it happens, we often say, "Wow, I've read and heard about God's love for years, but now *I really get it!*" That's the essence of Paul's prayer after his sweeping description of God's grace to choose, adopt, forgive, and seal us in Christ.

Paul begins his prayer with gratitude for his readers because he had "heard of your faith." This may seem strange since he was there for three years and undoubtedly knew many people in the church. Hadn't he seen their faith in person? There are two explanations. First, the message of the gospel had spread throughout that region, so Paul couldn't have known every person in every church in every community. He was being inclusive in his letter. But also, the letter probably was circulated to several cities in Asia and the surrounding areas. It was being sent to places Paul had never visited, but he had heard about them as he sat in prison in Rome. Whatever the case, Paul was thankful to hear the news that people had responded to the gospel message of forgiveness, hope, and love. In his gratitude, Paul again reminds them of the Trinitarian nature of God. He prayed that "the God of our Lord Jesus Christ, the Father of glory, may give you a spirit [or Spirit] of wisdom and revelation in the knowledge of him."

Spiritual perception isn't something we can manufacture. Blind people remain sightless until an outside agent—a surgeon or God—acts to give them the ability to see. Paul asks God to "enlighten the eyes of their hearts." I can't tell you how many times that has happened to me. I'm reading a passage or praying about a situation for the hundredth time, and a new insight flashes into my mind and heart. Suddenly or gradually, I have a new spiritual perception. Why didn't I see it before? Because I needed God to enlighten the eyes of my heart. In his most famous sermon, Jesus explained, "The eye is the lamp of the body. So, if your eye is healthy, your whole body will be full of light, but if your eye is bad, your whole body will be full of darkness. If then the light in you is darkness, how great is the darkness!" (Matthew 6:22-23) He wasn't talking about physical sight; he was talking about the devastating impact of spiritual blindness and the need for God to give us eyes to see the truth about him, our situations, and ourselves.

What do we need new eyes to see? Paul reflects back on what he had already written as preeminently important in the Christian life, and he asks God to convince the Ephesians of three crucial truths.

The hope of their calling

Some people think of the word 'calling' only in relation to vocational Christian service: A person is called to be a pastor or missionary or some other function in the church. That's not what Paul is talking about. We are called by God to be his chosen, beloved, forgiven children. He calls us to experience true life with Christ, now and for eternity. Our calling, though, came at great cost. We've been bought with a price, so we're no longer our own. If we grasp this fact, it will both thrill us and threaten us. We're amazed that the God of all wants to pour out his grace on us—who are inherently weak, selfish, defiant, and demanding. If we have a glimpse of our depravity (not just *how bad* we are, but *how bad off* we are), we'll be dancing for joy that God has forgiven us and loves us as much as he loves Jesus. But we also realize the experience of God's grace leads to complete surrender to his will. We are no longer the boss—he is. We no longer call the shots—he does. We no longer control our destiny—it's in his hands.

Like Jesus in the garden, our daily prayer is "not my will, but yours, Lord." And the ultimate hope of God's calling is to rule with him in his eternal kingdom. When time as we know it ends, and God makes everything right, we aren't going to sit on clouds strumming harps for endless days. The end of Revelation tells us heaven comes down to earth. We'll live a physical existence, with our bodies transformed to be like Christ's after his resurrection, and we'll have jobs to accomplish in his kingdom. That's our ultimate calling. We look forward to that day with eager anticipation.

The riches of his inheritance

Actually, hope and inheritance intersect in the new heaven and new earth. Paul asks God to open our eyes to see the glory of God's inheritance. His phrase could be taken two different ways: He might mean the fabulous inheritance we'll receive when we meet him face to face in glory, or he may be referring to the incredible concept that God feels rich because he has us as his children. We either receive a treasure, or we are a treasure. We can't miss!

If we take the first interpretation that Paul is praying that we'll anticipate a fabulous inheritance in the future, we realize we need to think more deeply about it. How would we act today if someone stole a hundred dollars from our purse or wallet but we were sure we'd receive ten billion dollars tomorrow? We might feel a bit inconvenienced, but we wouldn't be devastated. This monetary example can be amplified to include every kind of treasure: love, purpose, health, and time—in addition to walking streets of gold and having jeweled walls (which are John's best attempt to describe things that are beyond the powers of description). Do we believe this? Has it sunk into our hearts that the promise of our future is spectacular beyond words? It's true. Paul prays that we'll grasp this truth so deeply that we marvel at God's love and generosity.

The greatness of Christ's power

What does it mean to live as chosen, adopted, forgiven, and sealed children of the King? It means we are filled with hope, we look forward to our future, and we experience the power of God in everything we do. How much power? Paul layers words and concepts in a crescendo to convince us that the power available to each of us—right now—is the same power that raised Jesus Christ from the tomb! This power is absolute and complete. It was at work when Christ was seated at the right hand of God in heaven, and it is far above the unseen but very real supernatural forces of deception, temptation, and accusation we face today.

Some people claim authority over others, but they lack credibility to back it up. That's not the case with Jesus Christ. Paul makes the point that Christ's authority and power reigns now and for all time. The Father has put "all things under his feet." We may not grasp the significance of these words, but the Jews in the Ephesian church would instantly realize Paul is referring to the messianic psalm when David wrote, "The LORD says to my Lord: 'Sit at my right hand until I make your enemies your footstool'" (Psalm 110:1). Who has the power and authority to accomplish all Paul has described in this chapter? Jesus the sovereign King, that's who.

REAL RELATIONSHIPS

Too often, I hear people say they don't want to have anything to do with Jesus because "the church is filled with hypocrites." I wonder what these people really mean. I'm afraid they're referring to Christians who wear masks of perfect godliness and pleasant piety on Sunday mornings but act like the rest of the world the other 167 hours of the week. The first chapter of Ephesians invites us to be ruthlessly honest about our faults and flaws. God doesn't accept perfect people; he reaches out to warmly welcome those who have enough self-perception to admit they're guilty and rightly deserve only his condemnation. Those around us are looking for people with humble hearts, the willingness to be honest about our weaknesses and sins, and authentic faith in the grace of God. That's what I'm looking for, too.

Most of us can keep some of our sins and mistakes hidden, but pastors and other leaders take the risk of making blunders in plain sight. A few years ago, I wanted to change the blessing at the end of a worship service. I began the blessing—one that I'd given hundreds if not thousands of times before—but my mind went blank in the middle of it. I mumbled a few words and dismissed the people. I felt like a fool. I was so embarrassed. Several people came up to me and said, "Pastor, it was so good to see that you make mistakes like the rest of us." In that vulnerable moment, I'd become a bit more real to them, which opened the door to connect with them even more in the future.

The church needs to be a place where we can be brutally honest with one another, and then pour out the grace, hope, and power of God into each other's lives. Admitting our sins and struggles isn't hypocrisy—it's being honest that we're on the journey and we still have a long way to go. I think that's what people are looking for, and it's what Paul is advocating in the opening chapter of his letter.

Human beings have an almost limitless capacity for self-deception. We need people around us who are taking off their masks and who love us enough to point out the masks we still try to wear to cover up our vulnerability. We can be fully honest with God because he already knows everything about us, and we need to find a few people who love us enough to tell us the truth . . . especially when we don't want to hear it. We live in a fractured world. We can't expect every relationship and every situation to be nourishing and supportive, but we need a few—we desperately need a few. I believe we need three people: a Paul to mentor us, a Timothy we can lead and pour our lives into, and a Barnabas who will be our friend and supporter through the joys and difficulties of life. Without these people, we're just playing games in all our relationships, but with them, we grow strong in the grace of God. They are among God's greatest gifts to us.

Paul tells us from the beginning that God has blessed us "with every spiritual blessing." As he explains the gifts of grace to us, we're staggered by God's overwhelming, lavish love. If we're not, we don't yet get it.

At the end of each chapter, you'll find some questions. Take time to reflect on these and write your answers. Then, if you're in a Bible study or discussion group, share your thoughts with one another. God will use your conversations to sharpen your thinking and deepen your faith.

THINK ABOUT IT...

1. What do you hope to get out of this study of Paul's letter to the Ephesians?

2. Remember times when you were a child and people were being chosen for a team. How did you feel when you were picked? How did you feel when (and if) you were overlooked for a time? How did you feel as you waited?

3. How does the fact that God chose us (instead of us choosing him) give us security in our relationship with him? Does predestination confuse you or delight you? Explain your answer.

4. Do you know anyone who has adopted a child? Describe their experience of winning the child's trust. God could have forgiven us and made us slaves, but he made us his children. How does that affect our identity and motivations?

5. When is guilt a good thing? When is it debilitating? How does someone who is convinced of Christ's forgiveness think, feel, and act?

6. What are some evidences of the Holy Spirit's work in our lives?

7. How would you paraphrase Paul's prayer? How does it connect with the concepts of God's choosing, adoption, forgiveness, and the seal of the Spirit?

2

DYING TO LIVE

Ephesians 2:1-10

To live by grace means to acknowledge my whole life story,

the light side and the dark. In admitting my shadow side

I learn who I am and what God's grace means.

—Brennan Manning

When I was about 30 years old, I met a young couple, Mary and Tom, who lived near our church, and I invited them to worship with us. Mary began coming, but she came alone. I often saw her husband Tom going and coming from his house, but I didn't want to badger him about coming to church. We became friends and talked about everything under the sun. One day, I thought the time was right to ask the question: "Tom, I've noticed that you don't seem to be interested in coming to church with Mary. What's that about?"

He tilted his head a bit and screwed up his mouth, and then he pointed to his head and growled, "John, I've had religion up to here."

We were comfortable enough in our friendship for me to pursue it a bit further. I asked, "Tell me about your background. What happened that turned you off?"

He explained that he had been active in church when he was growing up, and in fact, he had begun to prepare to enter the ministry. He then explained, "But I quit because all I heard were rules—one after another, day after day. John, I had rules, laws, regulations, and demands up to my eyeballs, and I was sick of them! I couldn't stand it anymore, so I left the church." With a look of grave finality, he told me, "I haven't been back since."

I asked, "Is that what you think the Christian faith is about? Is it only rigid rules?"

"Yes," Tom nodded. "And I don't need that in my life."

I made a request: "Would you spend time with me so I can share the message of the gospel from the Bible with you? I think you'd be surprised—pleasantly surprised—by what you find there."

He said, "Yeah, I guess so."

Tom and I began meeting together on Saturday mornings to talk about God's grace and faith in Christ. He was like a sponge. He soaked up every passage that loudly proclaimed the wonder of God's unconditional love and forgiveness. About the third time we met, I told him, "Tom, do you realize that a relationship with God is entirely by God's grace? There's nothing we can do to earn His love. Following every rule perfectly doesn't do it. It's all him, not us." I quoted D. James Kennedy who explained that grace is "God's Riches At Christ's Expense." Tom liked the acronym. I told him that we can't do enough to earn God's acceptance or twist God's arm to love us. It's a free gift . . . ours for the taking. I talked about the *beauty* of Christ's death on the cross and explained that if we think it's all *duty*, we've missed God's heart.

After a few minutes, Tom looked up at me. He said softly, "John, that's too good to be true."

I smiled and assured him, "But Tom, it is true."

Tom trusted in the grace of Christ and became a passionate, dedicated follower. He was one of the most trusted lay leaders in our church—not because he was trying to prove anything to God or to anyone else, but because God had proven his love to him in the grace of Jesus Christ. Grace changes everything.

When we think the Christian life is all rules and no delight, we miss out on the abundance Christ wants us to experience. In *The Prodigal God*, author and pastor Tim Keller identifies several consequences of a misguided, rules-based Christianity:

> Every time something goes wrong in your life or a prayer goes unanswered, you wonder if it's because you aren't living right in this or that area. Another sign is that criticism from others doesn't just hurt your feelings, it devastates you. This is because your sense of God's love is abstract and has little real power in your life, and you need the approval of others to bolster your sense of value. You will also feel irresolvable guilt. When you do something you know is wrong, your conscience torments you for a long time, even after you repent. Since you can't be sure you've repented deeply enough, you beat yourself up over what you did. But perhaps the clearest symptom of this lack of assurance is a dry prayer life . . . there is no wonder, awe, intimacy, or delight in [your] conversations with God.[7]

Our experience of God's great grace begins in an odd place: the stark realization that we're utterly ruined and helpless without him.

DISMAL DESTINY

Without God, life makes no sense; it's empty and meaningless. When I was in my mid-20s, I wrestled for a while with the reality of God. I studied the philosophers and scientists (and even some theologians), and I concluded that life as we know it is probably the product of unguided evolutionary processes. It's all just chance and matter.

---

7   Tim Keller, *The Prodigal God* (Dutton: New York, 2008), pp. 63-64.

There is no God, and life has no ultimate meaning. Eventually, I had to face the consequences of nihilism: Nothing really matters. I hoped this conclusion would set me free from religion's expectations, but it scared the living daylights out of me! I remember feeling like I was backed up against a wall with God saying, "Okay, John, if this is what you believe, then live according to your beliefs." I realized Albert Camus and John Paul Sartre, two of the brightest people who had come to those conclusions, had committed suicide. I quickly realized that this dark night of my soul had better lead to some light—and quickly!

My journey back to faith began at the exact spot where Paul leads us next: the realization that we are hopeless and helpless apart from God. I had secretly suspected that Christianity was the domain of the weak. I wondered if a person could be bright, thinking, and reflective and still be a follower of Christ. The Lord led me to the writings of J. B. Phillips and C. S. Lewis, and my suspicions were quickly dashed. These men had sharp, refined intellectual gifts, and they wrote about Christ in ways that made my heart soar. Raw intelligence isn't a guarantee of finding truth. Some brilliant people are atheists, but some equally smart people have discovered that the truth of the Bible makes good sense—and a positive difference in the world.

At a conference in Britain, experts from across the globe debated the essence of the Christian faith. They compared the major religions of the world and the essential doctrines of Christianity. In what way, they asked, was Christ unique? Was it his incarnation? Other religions taught their gods appeared in human form. Was it the resurrection on Easter morning? Other faiths included accounts of people returning from the grave. The debate continued for a long time, and then C. S. Lewis walked into the room. He asked, "What's the rumpus about?"

Someone explained they were discussing Christianity's unique-ness. Lewis responded, "Oh, that's easy. It's grace."[8]

Grace isn't a prayer at dinner or a beautiful princess in Monaco. Grace is God's work to accomplish something we could never do for ourselves. Paul says we were hopeless, but God gave us a future. We were helpless, but God gave us power. We were dead, but God made us alive. He described the stark, dismal condition of people apart from Christ:

> And you were dead in the trespasses and sins in which you once walked, following the course of this world, following the prince of the power of the air, the spirit that is now at work in the sons of disobedience—among whom we all once lived in the passions of our flesh, carrying out the desires of the body and the mind, and were by nature children of wrath, like the rest of mankind (2:1-3).

Paul didn't say we need a little help to be right with God. We have absolutely nothing to offer him—not good works and not even good intentions. Dead people contribute nothing at all! They can't make themselves alive. The fact of our depravity, however, is terribly offensive to the human heart. We want to be somebody, to prove our-selves, to show that we're competent. We don't want to admit we can't make it on our own. However, Paul leaves no wiggle room for pride or misconception. He says we were under the authority of Satan, "the prince of the power of the air." We were members of his kingdom, not God's. And it wasn't like we wanted to do God's will and please him. Left to ourselves, we follow our selfish passions and desires. What

---

8   Cited by Philip Yancey in *What's So Amazing About Grace?* (Zondervan: Grand Rapids, 1997), p. 45.

did we deserve? Not grace. We were "by nature children of wrath." We deserved hell, "where their worm does not die and the fire is not quenched" (Mark 9:48).

We might wonder why Paul is painting such a bleak picture of human nature after his inspiring opening chapter. It doesn't make sense . . . or does it? Paul knows that we need to be utterly, repeatedly, and completely convinced of our depravity so we'll genuinely appreciate the wonderful grace of God. The default mode of the human heart isn't to trust in God's grace; it's to trust in our ability to earn God's favor by doing enough to impress him. Years ago, I read a book called *I Hurt Inside* by Ralph Underwager. He asks, "What causes psychological pain?" He answers, "It's always caused by our attempts to justify ourselves." We use people instead of loving them, grasp for all we can get, and put pleasure, possessions, and popularity in God's rightful place in our hearts. We trust in them instead of him, we delight in them instead of him, and we fear losing them instead of desiring to please him. These pursuits promise to give us power and love, but they drive us away from people and alienate us further from God.

We may think these verses describe only those who are addicts living under a bridge. That's not Paul's point at all. Apart from Christ, *every person* is hopelessly lost, dead, and unresponsive, unless God works the miracle of regeneration to give new life. There are people who sit in churches every week who think they're alive but are spiritually dead. They aren't thrilled with God's grace or awed by his majesty. They see God, in Larry Crabb's pithy phrase, as "a specially attentive waiter."[9] They expect him to serve them very well. When they like his service, they give him a tip of praise or money, but if he doesn't, they complain about his poor performance.

---

9   Larry Crabb, *Finding God*, (Zondervan: Grand Rapids, 1993), p. 18.

One of the biggest mistakes Christians make is treating God as a means instead of the ultimate end. Some of us pray, serve, and give in negotiations—as in a business relationship—with God to gain leverage to get what we want from him. In negotiations, both sides need something, but God, the creator of all, needs absolutely nothing from us. He gives, but he doesn't negotiate with us. When we treat God as a means, we get upset when we do our part but he doesn't come through on his end of the bargain. We need to realize that Jesus Christ is the Alpha and the Omega, the beginning and the end. We don't use him to get what we want. We love him, worship him, and stand in amazement at him as we learn more of who he really is.

I attended a conference for pastors of large churches a few years ago. The leaders asked us to share what God was doing in our ministries. People talked easily and with obvious excitement about their church's growth, new buildings, and new ministries. Each one, it seemed, was trying to outdo the others. As the sharing continued, something didn't sit right with me. Suddenly the question hit me: "Is God using us or are we using him?" It's a question I've needed to ask myself many times over the years. Is God only my waiter, my butler, or my assistant in my pursuit of power and prestige? If that's all he is, I'm no better than an atheist at a prestigious university or a pagan in the jungles of Africa. Jesus didn't come to assist me in my goals. He came to revolutionize my life. Even more, he came to offer me *real* life and transform my heart so I want to pursue his goals.

As people read Paul's description of those who are hopelessly lost, some might say, "Well, I believe in a loving God, not one who is harsh and would send people to hell."

I'd ask, "Do you believe in a God of justice?"

They often reply, "Oh yes, I do, but not a vengeful God. He loves everyone. He wouldn't punish anyone in hell."

I answer, "There's no contradiction between a God who is both loving and just. Love propels his justice to defend the helpless and punish the guilty, but his love also offers the grace of forgiveness for anyone who will take his hand." Hell is a reminder that God is just. The cross reminds us of his love and the penalty that had to be paid.

Some people have looked at God's love and justice, and they've told me, "God created quite a problem for himself. How can he love sinners and punish sin at the same time?"

I answer, "You're very perceptive. That's a great question, and it's one God has answered very clearly. Jesus Christ, the perfectly pure and righteous Son of God, stepped out of heaven to pay the price for our sins by dying on the cross. In that act, he demonstrated his love and suffered the judgment we deserved. He absorbed our debt and offers us a free gift of forgiveness and eternal life. How do we receive it? By grace though faith." That's where Paul turns now.

BUT GOD

My two favorite words in the Bible appear right here. My wife Elaine says the word 'but' is "an eraser word." When someone uses it, he's negating everything that came before it. That's exactly Paul's intention. Everything he has said in the first three verses is absolutely true, but God injects new revelation that overcomes those awful truths. After his description of doom and gloom for all people apart from Christ, things appear completely hopeless, but God intervenes and does what no one else could possibly do. Paul tells us:

> But God, being rich in mercy, because of the great love with
> which he loved us, even when we were dead in our trespasses,
> made us alive together with Christ—by grace you have been
> saved—and raised us up with him and seated us with him

in the heavenly places in Christ Jesus, so that in the coming ages he might show the immeasurable riches of his grace in kindness toward us in Christ Jesus. For by grace you have been saved through faith. And this is not your own doing; it is the gift of God, not a result of works, so that no one may boast (2:4-9).

Again, Paul piles up descriptive words and concepts in a torrent of excitement about God's grace. Some people think the study of theology is dry and boring. Paul surely wouldn't agree! He can hardly contain himself. I can envision him dictating this part of the letter with a huge smile on his face as he recounts the wonder of God's love and his decisive action to rescue sinners from sin, death, and hell. We had nothing to impress God, but he loved us anyway. We were dead, but God supernaturally made us alive. How far did God go to make us his own? Paul says we are "in him," raised from the grave and seated at the right hand of the Father. When we were baptized, we died "in Christ" and were raised "in him." The death and life of Jesus are imputed to us. It just doesn't get any better than that!

People who don't understand baptism think we're just throwing a little water on someone's head. They don't get it at all. When I explain the event before it happens, I tell them, "This sacrament institutes a mystical union. At a moment, this person is transported beyond time and space to be united with Christ—in his death, burial, and resurrection." (Paul beautifully captures this union in Romans 6.)

Typically, their eyes get big and they say something like this: "Wow, Pastor! We had no idea."

What is God's desire for those he loves? To show us "the immeasurable riches of his grace in kindness toward us in Christ Jesus." Did you get that? The creator of the universe delights in you and me so much that his purpose for the rest of eternity is to pour out his riches and convince us of his love and kindness. We often think of young couples who are captivated by each other's love. They spend time thinking of ways to surprise each other with little gifts and notes. Each love token cements the bond a little more. That's only a taste of the delight God enjoys as he showers his love and kindness on those he loves—you and me—now and for all eternity. Today, we have a taste of his grace and kindness, a down payment for the future, but someday, we'll receive our complete inheritance. The "riches of his grace" is a treasure beyond calculation, and each of us will receive it in full measure.

My grandfather once said, "When we get to heaven, there are going to be some real surprises. We'll find some people we were sure couldn't possibly be there, and some we expected to find will be missing. But the biggest surprise is to find that you're there. You don't deserve to be there. No one does. It's all about grace."

Do you wonder if God could love someone like you? The message of the gospel is that you don't have to have any credentials to earn his affection. It's a free gift of grace.

Are you afraid that your secret sins make you less than desirable? He loved you when you were dead, so you don't have to worry about his love for you now.

Do you think you still need to follow some rules to impress God? Please realize what you're saying and the contradiction between this thought and God's truth. Read this passage again and ask God to fill your heart with the wonder of grace.

When we read this part of the letter, it appears that Paul needed someone to proof his letter before he sent it out. He keeps saying "by grace" over and over again. But no, he doesn't need an English teacher to correct his work. He's making a point, one that we so easily miss even when it's repeated so often and so clearly. Two verses, eight and nine, repeat his point and add "not a result of works, so that no one may boast." If we believe we're accepted and acceptable by our efforts, then we feel arrogant when we are doing better than others, and we feel depressed when we realize we've failed to live up to our expectations. Without grace, we live on a roller coaster of pride and despair—and some of us make the cycle several times in a day!

Paul invites us to get off the wild ride and put our feet firmly on the grace of God. Actually, it's foolish and insulting for us to trust in our ability to win God's favor. To the Galatians, Paul explained, "I do not nullify the grace of God, for if righteousness were through the law, then Christ died for no purpose" (Galatians 2:21).

Since the time of Jesus and Paul, people have misunderstood the relationship between grace, faith, and works. Too often, people put works first. They think following the law (the rules, regulations, and demands of the Bible, churches, and conscience) is enough. As we've seen, that perception leaves people feeling superior or inferior, confused, and resentful. Obedience doesn't earn God's grace, but if we obey out of hearts of gratitude, our obedience pleases God. Our faith doesn't compel God to love us. Christ proved his love for us before we had any faith at all.

Grace comes first. We would never have faith if God didn't initiate his love toward us and make our hearts alive so we could love him in return. Faith then, is a gift from God so we can respond to him. Faith is the acknowledgment of what Jesus accomplished for us on the cross—he is both Savior and King. Even more, it is profound wonder at God's infinite greatness and grace. We don't *earn* a relationship with God by our works and obedience, but true faith always *produces* good works and obedience. Paul wrote the Corinthians about the necessary order of events, "For the love of Christ controls us, because we have concluded this: that one has died for all, therefore all have died; and he died for all, that those who live might no longer live for themselves but for him who for their sake died and was raised" (2 Corinthians 5:14-15). When we just follow rules, we live to impress people with how much we've done for them or for God, and we resent any insinuation that we haven't done enough. When the love of Christ floods our hearts, our motivations take a 180-degree turn. We delight in God, and we obey out of love and gratitude, not empty, oppressive, guilt-induced duty.

Dietrich Bonhoeffer was a spiritual lion in Germany during the years of Nazi tyranny. He stood up for Christ when the church wavered, and he conspired against Hitler in an attempt to rescue his nation. Bonhoeffer was under no illusions about the price of following Jesus. In his book, *The Cost of Discipleship*, he described the difference between anemic "cheap grace" and the life-changing power of "costly grace." He wrote,

> Cheap grace is the grace we bestow on ourselves. Cheap grace is the preaching of forgiveness without requiring repentance, baptism without church discipline, Communion without confession. . . . Cheap grace is grace without discipleship, grace without the cross, grace without Jesus Christ, living and incarnate. . . . Costly grace is the treasure hidden in the field; for the sake of it a man will gladly go and sell all that he has. It is the pearl of great price to buy which the merchant will sell all his goods. It is the kingly rule of Christ, for whose sake a man will pluck out the eye which causes him to stumble, it is the call of Jesus Christ at which the disciple leaves his nets and follows him.[10]

10 Dietrich Bonhoeffer, *The Cost of Discipleship* (Touchstone, 1995), pp. 45-49.

This is the gospel of Jesus Christ. We don't just need to reflect on it the day we trust him as our Savior. Paul reminds us that grace is the beginning point of a relationship with God, the motivation to obey him, and the truth that gives us hope in times of struggle. We need the gospel all day, every day.

Years ago a young man came to see me. He wanted to get married, and he asked me to officiate at the wedding. As we talked, I shared the gospel with him. I told him Christ came to earth to live and to die in our place to pay the penalty for our sins, and he was raised from the dead to prove all he had claimed was true and give us new life. I explained that we can have a personal relationship by grace through faith.

When I finished, he had a stunned look on his face. He exclaimed, "That's the gospel?"

I wasn't sure what to say, so I nodded, "Yes, that's the good news of Christ."

He told me, "Well, that's news to me. I always thought the gospel was a type of country music song."

When the gospel grips our hearts, we ask important (and much different) questions. We no longer focus on how we can impress God and others, and we don't feel compelled to hide our faults because we feel so ashamed. When we spend time with people, we don't suck them dry because we're desperately needy, and when we go to church, we want to give to God instead of only receiving from him. We live out of the overflow of our heartfelt experience of God's love, presence, and power.

It's so easy for people to get mixed up about grace, faith, and obedience. Our good works are visible and tangible, so we point to them when we want to justify ourselves, and we feel deeply ashamed when our failures scream that we're unworthy. In every walk of life, people look to accomplishments to prove themselves, but in God's kingdom, the pursuit of validation can get in the way of our experience of grace. Then, everything goes haywire. We then love, give, and serve, not to honor God and out of gratitude for grace, but to show others that we've arrived. There's a huge difference between piety and pietism. Piety is being filled with the love of God and serving out of full hearts. Pietism is a stern commitment to follow rules to prove ourselves. One is life; the other is death—we find both in church every Sunday.

Jesus and Jeremiah used familiar images of water to describe two approaches to spiritual life. At a great feast full of sacrifices and ceremonial washing, Jesus stood up and proclaimed, "If anyone thirsts, let him come to me and drink. Whoever believes in me, as the Scripture has said, 'Out of his heart will flow rivers of living water'" (John 7:37-38). The prophet Jeremiah described the people's misplaced pursuits as substituting stagnant, broken cisterns for the refreshment of living water. Through him God warned, "For my people have committed two evils: they have forsaken me, the fountain of living waters, and hewed out cisterns for themselves, broken cisterns that can hold no water" (Jeremiah 2:13). People haven't changed much since their day. We still try to use substitutes that leave us thirsty, empty, and confused. We wear a smile when we're dying inside because we don't want anyone to think less of us. We're jealous when others get attention, and we feel powerful when we compare ourselves to "those people" who don't follow the rules. We may read the Bible, pray, serve, and attend worship, but it's all a show. Checking off boxes of "godliness" and comparing ourselves with others always result in arrogance or despair—never peace, wisdom, and humility. Under this illusion, we spend all our time trying to mend the broken cisterns and "painting the empty well" instead of turning our attention to the true source of life and nourishment: God's love, forgiveness, and strength.

When we experience the extreme makeover of God's grace, the old tendencies to prove ourselves still remain rooted in our souls, but we have new resources of truth and grace to fight against them. The prophet Micah described the transformation of identity and motivation. He asked the right questions and found the right answers:

"With what shall I come before the Lord,
and bow myself before God on high?
Shall I come before him with burnt offerings,
with calves a year old?
Will the Lord be pleased with thousands of rams,
with ten thousands of rivers of oil?
Shall I give my firstborn for my transgression,
the fruit of my body for the sin of my soul?"
He has told you, O man, what is good;
and what does the Lord require of you
but to do justice, and to love kindness,
and to walk humbly with your God? (Micah 6:6-8)

What kind of good works do we think impress God and make up for our sins? What would catch his eye and win some credit? Few of us would consider such extravagant offerings as "thousands of rams," "ten thousands of rivers of oil," or our firstborn child. But these expensive sacrifices aren't what God wants from us. He wants us to respond to his great grace with gratitude and humility, to take action to protect the poor and disadvantaged, to be kind to those around us, and walk before God with thankful hearts, ready to do whatever he asks because we want to show him how much we love him. Jesus, Jeremiah, Micah, and Paul used different word pictures, but it's the same powerful message of grace.

In his famous book, *Games People Play*, Eric Burns identifies 70 ways people try to manipulate each other instead of living in truth and love. These games, he asserts, aren't fun. They are designed to control the perceptions and behaviors of those we don't really trust, such as God, our families, our co-workers, and even ourselves. Burns defines relational games as "a recurring set of transactions often repetitive, superficially rational, with a concealed motivation; or, more colloquially, as a series of transactions with a snare, or gimmick."[11] These games always have a payoff: They gain attention, win applause, avoid conflict, or manipulate others in some way. Using good works to earn God's approval is playing a manipulative game with him. It dishonors him, discounts Christ's sacrifice, and puts us in control of the relationship. Using good deeds to impress people also devalues them, keeps them at arm's length, and is inherently manipulative instead of loving.

If you've been playing games (and all of us have in some way or another), be honest about them. Turn to Jesus, admit your false pursuits, and invite him to flood your heart with his marvelous grace. Nothing else will do.

MASTERPIECE

Real faith always produces genuine desire to please God. It never leaves us passive and complacent. Paul caps off all the glowing statements of our new identity in Christ when he writes: "For we are his workmanship, created in Christ Jesus for good works, which God prepared beforehand, that we should walk in them" (2:10).

The Greek word translated "workmanship" means "masterpiece." When I wrestled with the nature of God when I was a young man, I sometimes considered the possibility that human beings might be the

---

11   Eric Burns, *Games People Play* (Ballantine Books, 1996).

product of random collections of atoms. I couldn't have been more wrong. We have been created and crafted by the Master Artist. Every human being has inherent dignity, but those who have trusted in Christ are masterpieces of his creation *and* his redemption. No one is junk. No one is a throwaway. People who have embraced Christ's forgiveness are shaped like a Michelangelo and painted like a Rembrandt. But great artists don't do the same work over and over again. Each of us is God's unique masterpiece. We're very different, with varied skills, personalities, passions, and experiences, and God uses each of us for a particular purpose.

Your personality isn't an accident. Your appearance isn't a joke. Your talents aren't the product of random events. God considers you to be his masterpiece. When he looks at you, he stands back and smiles. But he doesn't leave us on the wall. He created and crafted us to be his partners in the greatest enterprise the world has ever known. We're *junior* partners, that's for sure, but partners nonetheless. Everywhere we go, we represent the King and Savior. We're his ambassadors in the boardroom and the bedroom, the office and the school, the backyard and the worship service.

Have you noticed how many times Paul puts God's present work in our lives in the context of eternity? We may think today is all there is, but God lives outside time. He sees it all from the beginning to the end. He chose us before time began, and we have a promised inheritance when time ends. We may go to class to learn a new leadership or management technique, but God began preparing us to be his partners long ago. God has a magnificent, sweeping plan to make all things right and unite everything under Christ's rule, and he has chosen us to participate in his purposes. Every one of us is divinely chosen to be part of God's plan. We all play important roles in God's redemptive process to transform individuals, families, and cultures. Is there any higher honor? Is there any greater challenge?

Grace, faith, and then works. We need to remember the order. When grace captures our hearts, it awakens genuine faith, which always results in gratitude, wonder, joy, and obedience. The church father Ambrose observed, "Faith is the mother of a good will and right doing."

Has Paul's description of our utter hopelessness and the magnificent grace of God stirred your heart as you've read this chapter? I believe we appreciate grace only in proportion to our grasp of our depravity. If we still think we can do some things to earn points with God, we won't see our desperate need for God's forgiving love. When Martin Luther breathed his last breath, he said, "We are all beggars; that is true." Do you see yourself as a beggar or a negotiator? If you're a beggar, the message of grace makes your heart sing! If you're a negotiator, it bores you and leaves you flat.

Quite often, people greet me and say, "Hey, Pastor. How are you doing?"

I answer, "A whole lot better than I deserve."

They sometimes try to correct me, "Pastor, you shouldn't say that."

I almost laugh. "Oh yes, I should. You don't know me the way God knows me. He knows very well what I deserve, but he's given me his grace. That's infinitely better than I deserve."

Be brutally honest about the darkness in your heart. God already knows, he forgives, he has claimed you as his own, and he has a marvelous purpose for you.

THINK ABOUT IT...

1. If a person believes he has to earn God's love by doing enough good things, how does this perspective shape his response to God, his motivations, and his relationships with others? How does he respond to success and failure?

2. Why is it essential that Christians grasp the truth about their depravity (in verses 1-3)? In this passage, what descriptive phrases stand out to you? What do they mean to you?

3. In verse 4, how is 'but' an eraser word? How do the following verses erase the painful facts of our depravity?

4. In verses 5-7, what is Paul saying by all his statements of "in him" and "with him"?

5. How would you paraphrase verse 7?

6. Explain the connection between (and order of) grace, faith, and works.

7. Think about the passages from John, Jeremiah, and Micah. What are some empty substitutes people try to use? Why don't they work?

8. Do you really believe you are God's masterpiece? Why or why not? How does it affect people who genuinely believe this fact?

3

MYSTERIOUS EMBRACE

Ephesians 2:11-3:21

Often we have no time for our friends

but all the time in the world for our enemies.

—Leon Uris

To God, human relationships are incredibly important. The Bible knows nothing of the American ideal of "rugged individualism." Connections matter. In fact, the way Christians relate to each other is (or at least can be) one of the brightest lights of God's love. If we fail to love each other, the world has a right to wonder if Christ makes even a dent in our lives. Jesus told his disciples, "A new commandment I give to you, that you love one another: just as I have loved you, you also are to love one another. By this all people will know that you are my disciples, if you have love for one another" (John 13:34-35). Immediately after Paul describes the wonder of God's grace to give life to those who are spiritually dead, he explains that a surefire evidence of this grace is our love for Christians who are different from us—ethnically, socially, culturally, and economically. Loving people this way, though, often comes with a price tag.

In 1974, the Vietnam War was over. Helicopters took the last flights from the roof of the United States Embassy in Saigon, leaving thousands behind. Soon, boatloads of people sailed to Thailand and the islands of Indonesia. And hundreds of refugees eventually made it to the area of Galveston Bay near our church. Many of these Vietnamese people had been fishermen before, and they scraped enough money together to enter the shrimping business in Kemah. The shrimpers who had spent a lifetime building their businesses were outraged at the competition, and they enlisted the aid of a few members of the Ku Klux Klan. The Klan led marches and posted notices threatening the Vietnamese people. Their message was simple: "Get out! This is our area of the Bay and the Gulf, and you're not welcome!"

Tensions in the community ran high. The KKK, of course, claims to represent Christ and his purposes. Their message of exclusion and hatred confused many and offended most. I joined several pastors in the area to co-sign a letter published in the local newspaper that confronted the hypocrisy of the Klan's rage and intimidation while they claimed to reflect the will and nature of Jesus Christ. We didn't just write a letter—we took action. Our church was instrumental in helping over 100 refugees settle in this area. It wasn't enough to stand up against injustice; we also stood by those who needed our help. In our home, we knew we might pay a steep price. Elaine was terrified that she'd wake up and find a cross burning on our front lawn. Thank God, cooler heads prevailed and the tensions eased.

One of the families that came from Southeast Asia was from Laos. The couple somehow had brought the husband's mother with them on the boat to freedom, and they eventually came to our community. When they arrived, they needed a place to stay. A man who was the top executive in Lockheed Martin and his wife opened their home and invited them to come. One day I went to visit them. I'll never forget the picture. The elderly mother sat in a chair as her daughter-in-law knelt on a rug in front of her, rubbing one of her feet to keep her warm. The executive's wife was on the floor next to the daughter-in-law rubbing the old woman's other foot. This scene was a powerful, living image of God's love and kindness. I've never forgotten being in the room with them that day.

When the grace of God captures our hearts, we care about the things he cares for, and our hearts break over the things that break his heart. We can't manufacture these values and passions. The Spirit of God produces them in us, and they become "the fruit of the Spirit." As God kneads his grace into us, we learn to love like Jesus loves (1 John 4:10-11), we forgive like Jesus forgives (Ephesians 4:32), and we accept people the way Jesus accepts them (Romans 15:7). Gradually, our lives become an extension of his. We're still flawed in our sinful desires and inordinate fears, but gradually we become a little more like Jesus in our thoughts, words, and deeds.

DRAWING LINES

We don't have to look far to expose prejudice and suspicion between groups of people. It's human nature to draw lines between "those people" and ourselves—we think of people as insiders or outsiders. We inscribe these lines according to ethnicity, race, education, socio-economic status, politics, doctrine, clothes, and where people live—among other things. We believe we're "better than" and they're "less than." Our air of superiority (or inferiority, depending on which side of the line we're on and our perception of the other side) fuels suspicion and resentment.

Sometimes, we're the victims of other people drawing lines and making assumptions. When Elaine and I came to Gloria Dei, we lived in a house near the church in Nassau Bay. When some young people found out where we lived, a few of them backed away because they assumed we were snobs and felt superior to anyone who didn't live there.

It was obvious they didn't know us very well! At the time, our children were in school. They caught the brunt of the suspicions. I remember sitting at dinner and talking about their classmates' misperceptions. One of them exclaimed, "Dad, don't they know we're just like every-body else?"

Our kids went to a high school where they mixed with all races and economic groups. I'm so glad they had that experience. It gave them respect for all people and the ability to relate to anyone anywhere.

I hate to say it, but Christians—even Christian leaders—often are no different from anyone else in poisoning relationships with an air of superiority. I've been to denominational conventions when doctrinal issues were being debated, and I heard church leaders hooting, holler-ing, booing, and yelling catcalls at those with whom they disagreed. It made me physically sick. Jesus came "full of grace and truth"—not one or the other, but both. It's perfectly right to talk about the issues of doctrine and truth, but we need to respect those who disagree with us, and beyond that, to love them the way Jesus loves us—deeply, inten-tionally, and graciously. Instead of tearing down walls that divide us, some Christians erect higher walls, and in a few cases, seem to want to man them with machine guns!

Comparison kills. Feeling superior or inferior to other groups or classes of people may be a normal aspect of human nature, but it is a lethal poison in the body of Christ. Paul wastes no time in address-ing the dividing line between two groups who traditionally despised each other. If the grace of God was going to make a difference in an individual's life, it also had to radically redefine relationships. In his day, Jews and Gentiles were openly hostile to one another. It wasn't just preference; it was long-simmering, fierce animosity. The big ques-tion in the early church was, "Can Gentiles be Christians?" And if the answer was "Yes," under what conditions? Both groups were sitting in the church in Ephesus. Paul had been with them for about three years, and he had undoubtedly spoken often and eloquently about the power of the gospel to bring warring people together. In his letter, he articulated his point from several angles:

Therefore remember that at one time you Gentiles in the flesh, called "the uncircumcision" by what is called the circumcision, which is made in the flesh by hands—remember that you were at that time separated from Christ, alienated from the commonwealth of Israel and strangers to the covenants of promise, having no hope and without God in the world. But now in Christ Jesus you who once were far off have been brought near by the blood of Christ. For he himself is our peace, who has made us both one and has broken down in his flesh the dividing wall of hostility by abolishing the law of commandments expressed in ordinances, that he might create in himself one new man in place of the two, so making peace, and might reconcile us both to God in one body through the cross, thereby killing the hostility. And he came and preached peace to you who were far off and peace to those who were near. For through him we both have access in one Spirit to the Father. So then you are no longer strangers and aliens, but you are fellow citizens with the saints and members of the household of God, built on the foundation of the apostles and prophets, Christ Jesus himself being the cornerstone, in whom the whole structure, being joined together, grows into a holy temple in the Lord. In him you also are being built together into a dwelling place for God by the Spirit (2:11-22).

In the first century, many Jewish Christians had a checklist. Gentiles could be accepted in the church, they believed, under the same conditions they were accepted into the Jewish community—if they were circumcised and followed God's commandments. Paul is saying, "No, it's different in the church. Jesus changes everything! It's not by rules and regulations. Our relationships with each other are based on the same thing as our relationship with God—it's all about grace."

To make his point, Paul uses the imagery of the temple. Jewish men could worship in the center section, and the women were separated from them. Still farther out was the court of the Gentiles, which was surrounded by walls warning Gentile converts not to go any nearer. Paul said that Jesus has broken down the dividing wall between people and eliminated the laws that prevented the two groups from mixing. Paul was no Pollyanna. He recognized the inherent distrust and hatred between the groups, and he said Jesus' death on the cross effectively "killed the hostility." Isn't that a strange and wonderful concept? Christ's death killed our hatred for others! Too often, we tolerate hostility between others and ourselves. Paul says that God didn't wink at relational conflict and superiority. Jesus paid the ultimate price in his sacrifice on the cross—for individuals to come to faith in him, yes, but also so that bridges of grace, hope, and love could be built between us. That's how we show the love of God to the world. When they see us bickering among ourselves, they have every right to wonder if our faith is real.

In place of natural and long-standing resentment, entitlement, and suspicion, Jesus creates a new sense of unity. Paul uses two powerful metaphors: a family and a building. As believers, we all have one Father, so every Christian is part of God's household. We may get to pick our friends, but we don't have the option to pick our brothers and sisters. We're in it with them whether we like it or not! Our new, transformed relationships create a different kind of temple—not one made from stones, but built on the cornerstone of Jesus Christ. This was a radical concept to the people reading Paul's letter. In this letter, Paul explained that the new temple, God's presence in his people, includes everyone who trusts in Jesus—no exceptions. Each believer is a temple, and together, we form a far bigger, more formidable temple to shine the light of God to the world. This building, though, has an unusual quality: It grows! As we love one another, we grow deeper into the grace of God, and more people are attracted and added to the edifice.

To both Jews and Gentiles, Paul's description of the body of believers as God's temple was very important. A temple is where heaven and earth meet. In the Jewish temple, God's presence was found in the Holy of Holies. It was the most revered place on earth. When Jesus died, the veil of the inner sanctum was torn from top to bottom, signifying that all people now have access to God through faith in Jesus Christ. Now, Paul is saying that we not only have access to God's presence, we actually are God's holy temple where the Spirit lives and where heaven and earth meet! But God isn't finished building this temple. It will continue until the end of the ages when Christ returns and all things are made right. Until then, it is our privilege and responsibility to create loving, supportive relationships in which the light of the world shines for all to see.

Where does God show up to do his work of kingdom building? In the relationships of his people as we love God with all our hearts, love our neighbors as ourselves, and love "the least of these" who might easily be overlooked.

I often think back to the original temple in Jerusalem. David wanted to build it, but God said he was a warrior, not a builder. His son Solomon built an incredible building for God. It was carefully crafted of the finest materials and the most skilled workmanship. When it was dedicated, Solomon pulled out all the stops. He sacrificed 22,000 oxen and 120,000 sheep (1 Kings 8:62-63)! But on the day God inaugurated his new family, he paid an even higher price and made a more extravagant display. He sacrificed the blameless, holy Son of God for you and me.

Solomon's temple was grand and glorious, but the temple of God's family is different. There are bricks that don't seem to fit quite right and joints that seem out of place. Still, we're held together by something more substantial than mortar and bronze. We're joined together by the love of God.

NOTHING NEW

In our day, many people in churches are vocal about their "rights" and their political opinions about minority groups who "take our services and spend our taxes." The rhetoric is so caustic that I wonder if some of these people have listened to themselves. They thrive on radio talk shows that fuel suspicion and resentment. Certainly, we need good policies that address the problems, but Christians need to remember the message of the gospel. God loves insiders, outsiders, and upside-downers. He loves everyone, and he seems to give special attention to those who are most often overlooked. A true test of our faith is the depth of our love for these people. Paul didn't come up with this concept out of the blue. When God called Abraham, he promised to make him a blessing so that "in you all the families of the earth shall be blessed" (Genesis 12:3). A millennium later, God's people were finally in the land God had promised Abraham. God, though, wasn't content to let their focus become ingrown. The psalmist wrote,

Sing to the Lord, bless his name;

    tell of his salvation from day to day.

Declare his glory among the nations,

    his marvelous works among all the peoples! (Psalm 96:2-3)

God's love reaches out to all people from all nations and all classes. The prophet Zechariah recorded God's heart: "Thus says the Lord of hosts, Render true judgments, show kindness and mercy to one another, do not oppress the widow, the fatherless, the sojourner, or the poor, and let none of you devise evil against another in your heart" (Zechariah 7:9-10). In , author and pastor Tim Keller applies this passage to our culture:

> In premodern, agrarian societies, these four groups [in Zechariah 7] had no social power. They lived at subsistence level and were only days from starvation if there was any famine, invasion, or even minor social unrest. Today this quartet would be expanded to include the refugee, the migrant worker, the homeless, and many single parents and elderly people.[12]

God shows special care for "the least of these," and he expects us to care for them, too. When we feel superior or inferior to individuals or groups of people, we find fault in anything and everything they say and do. In fact, we delight in pointing out their flaws. Putting them down makes us feel powerful, but it tears down bridges. Princeton professor Miroslav Volf survived the Balkan War and saw the horrors of ethnic hatred firsthand. Real relationships, he asserts, begin with authentic forgiveness. In *Exclusion and Embrace*, he observed,

---

12 Timothy Keller, *Generous Justice* (Dutton: New York, 2010), p. 4.

Forgiveness flounders because I exclude the enemy from the community of humans even as I exclude myself from the community of sinners. But no one can be in the presence of the God of the crucified Messiah for long without overcoming this double exclusion—without transposing the enemy from the sphere of the monstrous . . . into the sphere of shared humanity and herself from the sphere of proud innocence into the sphere of common sinfulness. When one knows [as the cross demonstrates] that the torturer will not eternally triumph over the victim, one is free to rediscover that person's humanity and imitate God's love for him. And when one knows [as the cross demonstrates] that God's love is greater than all sin, one is free to see oneself in the light of God's justice and so rediscover one's own sinfulness.[13]

Bridges of love are built only on grace. Everything else is games, manipulation, fear, assumptions, and the desire to be one-up on others. Peter wrote, "Love covers a multitude of sins" (1 Peter 4:8). I've learned that lesson many times. Many years ago on a Sunday morning, I got up to teach an adult Bible class and saw a hippie couple sitting in the group. My instant reaction (as I opened God's word for the people) was, "Oh no, not *those* people!" I had never met them, but I stereotyped them the moment I saw them. They kept coming to our church, trusted Christ as their Savior, and became wonderful servants in our congregation. I had misread them entirely. From them, I learned that no one is beyond the grace of God, and I learned that my hard heart needs to be softened by God's love for all people.

---

13   Miroslav Volf, *Exclusion and Embrace* (Abingdon Press: Nashville, 1996), 124.

On another occasion, a young man appeared in our offices. He looked like he'd been traveling for weeks with little food and without a shower. He had only what he carried in his backpack. I'd learned my lesson from the hippie couple, so I befriended this young man. I helped him get some dental care he desperately needed, and we spent time together. After a couple of days, it was Friday. He asked, "Pastor, would it be okay for me to sleep in the alcove of the chapel? I'd like to come to your services Sunday, but I don't have anywhere to stay the next two nights." I was happy to let him sleep there.

Early Sunday morning, I arrived at church and looked for him. I couldn't find him anywhere. I saw one of our long-time members and asked, "Hey Jim, have you seen a young man around here?"

I realized it wasn't a very specific question. We had lots of "young men" at the church, but I thought he might realize this young man was somewhat unique. He looked indignant and explained, "I sure did, Pastor. He had been sleeping in the alcove. I told him to get his ass out of here! And he did."

I was heartbroken. I told him, "Jim, I gave him permission to sleep there. He was going to worship with us today." He looked at me like I'd lost my mind. He just shrugged and walked off.

Sometimes we exclude people intentionally, but we may exclude them simply because we don't notice they exist. Many people have moved to the suburbs to avoid crime, noise, and congestion of the cities, but too often, we live in homogeneous neighborhoods that lack the varied colors and rich textures of a more complex fabric of relationships. We've fled to safety and convenience, but at the expense of not rubbing shoulders with a lot of people Jesus loves.

PAUL'S STORY

One of the most interesting aspects of this part of Paul's letter is that it was penned by a man who had been the most rigid, self-righteous, judgmental, arrogant, spiteful Jew the world has ever known! Before he met Christ on the road to Damascus, Paul was the top dog in Judaism, and he proved his zeal by arresting and executing Christians. If anyone ever demonstrated a changed attitude toward other ethnic groups, it was Paul. If others resisted and said, "Yeah, but you don't understand how hard it is to love those people," Paul could say, "Oh yes, I do. I understand better than you can possibly imagine. If I can love them and accept them, you can, too."

Paul, the toughest guy on the block, had been touched by the grace of God. Instead of despising outsiders, God filled his heart with love for them. Instead of overlooking them, Paul went out of his way to raise money to care for them. Instead of feeling comfortable with seemingly intractable, age-old animosities, Paul addressed them head-on to correct them. It wasn't enough to maintain the status quo and see if God worked to replace hatred with love. Paul taught, modeled, and acted decisively to build a new family on the solid rock of God's grace, mercy, kindness, and love.

In Paul's letter, he stepped back to share his personal story and his perception of his role in the drama. Paul invites us to use him as an example. Another good model for us is the former slave ship captain John Newton, who became one of the leaders of the church in the 19th century in England. His hymn, "Amazing Grace," has blessed Christians for generations. People who have sinned greatly sometimes appreciate grace more than the rest of us. However, if we all had a clear glimpse of the darkness in our hearts, we'd realize we're all deeply flawed and terribly stained by sin. Some have committed overt sins of addictions, adultery, lying, stealing, and wild living. But many others have committed "the sins of the overly righteous"—arrogance, being judgmental, and living in bitterness. All of us need the cleansing, healing, life-changing grace of God.

In the first century, people who read the Scriptures realized God had a plan to work in the lives of Gentiles, but no one guessed that God's plan was to include them as equal partners. No insiders and outsiders. No one who was "one up" while others were "one down." By the grace of God, all believers were chosen, adopted, forgiven, and sealed. That was revolutionary! It had been a "mystery," but Paul explained it so everyone would understand. You can imagine how both groups may have responded as the letter was read. The Gentiles probably shouted for joy, and the Jews realized they had to move over and make room for people they had despised for centuries. No one could have dreamed that God would welcome outsiders as full members of his family, but he does. Paul wrote:

> For this reason I, Paul, a prisoner for Christ Jesus on behalf of you Gentiles—assuming that you have heard of the stewardship of God's grace that was given to me for you, how the mystery was made known to me by revelation, as I have written briefly. When you read this, you can perceive my insight into the mystery of Christ, which was not made known to the sons of men in other generations as it has now been revealed to his holy apostles and prophets by the Spirit. This mystery is that the Gentiles are fellow heirs, members of the same body, and partakers of the promise in Christ Jesus through the gospel.
>
> Of this gospel I was made a minister according to the gift of God's grace, which was given me by the working of his power.

To me, though I am the very least of all the saints, this grace
was given, to preach to the Gentiles the unsearchable riches of
Christ, and to bring to light for everyone what is the plan of
the mystery hidden for ages in God who created all things, so
that through the church the manifold wisdom of God might
now be made known to the rulers and authorities in the heavenly places. This was according to the eternal purpose that he
has realized in Christ Jesus our Lord, in whom we have bold-
ness and access with confidence through our faith in him. So
I ask you not to lose heart over what I am suffering for you,
which is your glory (3:1-14).

This part of Paul's letter was intimate and self-revealing. He assures them, "Hey, I didn't come up with the message of the gospel of
grace over coffee this morning. It was God's divine plan all along."
God revealed it to him, and he passed it on to everyone he met . . . on
the road, in synagogues, in homes, on ships, and everywhere else.

Paul had been arrogant; now he was suffering for Christ. He had
been a recognized leader; now he was a prisoner. He had endured every kind of ridicule and deprivation so the gospel could touch more
lives. Love propelled him to suffer for Christ and so others could know
God's grace. Helmut Thielicke was a theologian and the author of *The
Trouble with the Church*. He wrote, "Tell me how much you know of
the sufferings of your fellow men, and I will tell you how much you
have loved them."[14] People knew Paul loved them because he had suffered for them.

The question each of us has to ask is this: Do I really believe the
gospel of Jesus Christ? If others can't tell a difference in our attitudes

---

14   Cited by Bruce Barton in *The Life Application Bible Commentary: 1, 2 &
3 John* (Tyndale House, 2001), p. 75.

and behaviors, then maybe we're just going through the motions. The problem, though, isn't always with the people sitting in the congregations. After visiting the United States, Thielicke concluded that there are too many preachers in America who don't believe a word of what they say on Sunday morning. Another author who made a similar observation is Pierre Berton, who wrote *The Comfortable Pew*. After studying the church in America, he observed that people walk into and out of church each week without any real life change because they don't understand the life-changing message of the gospel.

I was born in Walburg, Texas, and I grew up there and in San Antonio. My father was a Lutheran schoolteacher and principal. Our home was rooted in God's truth and love, but I was a product of the times. I didn't try to become a racist. It wasn't my aspiration in any way, but I was one anyway. I was content for blacks to remain on their side of the tracks, and the Hispanics should stay in their neighborhoods. No one taught me to look down on them. It was entirely normal and natural, but I was so wrong. I heard the gospel over and over again, but it wasn't making a dent in my attitudes toward "those people." Paul's letter shows how God got my attention, and he's trying to get yours, too.

MAKING IT REAL

In the first chapter, Paul prayed to ask God to make our new identity real to us. Here, he prays again. This time, he asks God to make his love so rich and dynamic in our lives that it spills out into every relationship. He reflects back on God's call to Abraham to bless every family on earth, and then he articulates our hearts' greatest desire. He wrote,

> For this reason I bow my knees before the Father, from whom every family in heaven and on earth is named, that according to the riches of his glory he may grant you to be strengthened

with power through his Spirit in your inner being, so that Christ may dwell in your hearts through faith—that you, being rooted and grounded in love, may have strength to comprehend with all the saints what is the breadth and length and height and depth, and to know the love of Christ that surpasses knowledge, that you may be filled with all the fullness of God.

Now to him who is able to do far more abundantly than all that we ask or think, according to the power at work within us, to him be glory in the church and in Christ Jesus throughout all generations, forever and ever. Amen.

Paul was praying for you and me! I want the Holy Spirit to work with power in the depths of my heart to give me strength so I'm not easily threatened by superficial differences with others. I want Christ to be perfectly at home in me, so he has full access to every fear, hope, and desire. I want to know him and experience his love—not superficially, but the breadth, length, height, and depth of his kindness and grace. I want to be so assured of the wonderful doctrines of grace that they sink deep into my heart and transform every part of my life. Then, and only then, will I be filled and overflowing with the presence, peace, pardon, and purpose of Jesus Christ.

Zig Ziglar once asked people at a seminar, "Do you know the most powerful nation in the world? It's the imagine-nation." Paul's doxology asks us to imagine what God might do in our lives and relationships. It's an explosion of praise and hope that blacks will love whites, Republicans will love Democrats, and rich people will love the poor. When our circumstances look dark, when our relationships are on the brink of disaster, and when we're about to lose hope, we need to remember that nothing is impossible for God. His power and love open doors. And it's all for his glory—because he's the one who deserves every honor we can give him.

BEYOND TOLERATION

Transformation is both inevitable and difficult. It's inevitable because it's the nature of growth for seeds of faith to sprout and grow strong and healthy, but heart change is difficult because we have to fight against powerful forces, including "the rulers and authorities in the heavenly places," the world's values that are communicated in every advertisement, and our selfish human desires. We may experience a wonderful, dramatic conversion or a growth spurt at some point in our Christian experience, but true growth comes gradually from thousands of small choices to pick God's will and ways instead our own. Jesus told his disciples, "If anyone would come after me, let him deny himself and take up his cross and follow me. For whoever would save his life will lose it, but whoever loses his life for my sake will find it" (Matthew 16:24-25). This lifestyle may or may not begin with a dramatic choice, but it is shaped by countless smaller decisions every day.

A heart is changed by grace and courageous steps of love; both are essential if we are to apply Paul's truth and experience the answer to his prayer. Too often, we settle. We're complacent with the status quo because reaching out to others seems too difficult, too time-consuming, and too threatening to our security. It may feel good to take old clothes to a homeless shelter, but what if those people want to be our friends?

Let me ask a few questions:

- How much love for others is "good enough" to you?
- What's the limit of your willingness to sacrifice for others?

- What does it mean to genuinely love people of other races, cultures, and groups?
- How much of your life is spent in the quest for safety instead of demonstrations of God's love?

And now, let me make some suggestions:

Avoid generalizations.

Don't begin sentences with "Asians are . . ." or "Hispanics always . . ." or "White people certainly. . . ." Stereotyping people may have some basis in statistical analysis, but generalizations demean people and prevent us from seeing an individual's unique hopes, fear, and needs. Let sociologists and politicians make broad assumptions about groups and classes of people. You and I are called by God to see each person as inherently valuable and unique.

Ask questions . . . and listen.

When we make assumptions about people, we run great risks of offending them. If we love people, we'll ask questions, and we'll keep asking deeper and deeper questions as the relationship develops. It's not an inquisition—it's a friendship. Invest in it, and listen carefully to the person's answers. They might surprise you, and they'll definitely inform you. When we don't ask questions, all we have are our preconceived assumptions.

Value differences.

Too often, we despise differences instead of delighting in them. Some of us walk into a conversation with someone from another culture or denomination and look for a fight! Wouldn't life be dull if everyone ate the same food and believed exactly the same things?

Learn to appreciate different perspectives. Not as many things are black and white or right and wrong as some of us believe.

Recognize superiority and inferiority.

I don't know anyone whose heart doesn't have at least some prejudice lurking beneath the surface—and many of us proudly wear our prejudices! How sad. We won't make much progress in the transformation of our attitudes if we don't realize our flaws of superiority and inferiority. As we talk to people (or talk about them), we need to take our own temperature and see how hot we're running. If we start to "get big" (demanding, angry, and loud), we need to back off and calm down. If we notice we're "getting little" (weak, quiet, and intimidated), we need to sit up and speak up. Repentance starts with honesty.

Watch the political rhetoric.

I believe our country is the greatest ever founded on earth, but we need to be careful in how we exercise our right of free speech. Too often, I hear Christians loudly, angrily, and passionately arguing for or against particular positions. That's their right, but they need to stop and listen to themselves. God has called us to live in grace and truth. Jesus said some harsh things to the Pharisees, but he loved them so much he was willing to go to their houses for dinner, and he was willing to die for them. Policies like the national debt, access to healthcare, and immigration are red flag issues. Pray, ask God for wisdom, listen to opposing positions, and find a way to talk about these issues that doesn't offend others.

Treat people like brothers and sisters.

This may not be a positive statement for some of us! We need to remember that all believers—Lutherans and Pentecostals, Baptists and Episcopalians—are part of God's eternal family. He's our Father and Lord. The way we treat other Christians delights or grieves God's heart, and it shapes the lives of those who are watching. In love, Christ reaches out to everyone. Do we?

Years ago, I attended a church growth conference at Fuller Theological Seminary in California. Pastors and church leaders from many denominations were there. At the time, I was a rigid, dyed-in-the-wool Lutheran. I was deeply suspicious of anyone who couldn't quote Luther at the drop of a hat about any subject imaginable. At one point, I met with the leader, Peter Wagner, and privately communicated my concerns about some of the other men at the event. He immediately commented, "Kieschnick, we've got plenty of concerns about you Lutherans, too!" I was shocked, but I was determined to see what God had for me there. Soon, I discovered that I had made mountains out of molehills. Many of the negative assumptions I'd made about the leaders from other denominations simply weren't true. In his book, , Martin Marty said that anytime we generalize about a group of people, we violate the eighth commandment to avoid false witness against our neighbor. Ouch!

In the church, we spend far too much time building walls instead of bridges. Instead, we need to realize that the death of Christ broke down the walls that divide us. His love binds us together, but it doesn't make us a homogeneous blob. We retain the richness of our cultures, and we bring our differences into relationships of love, forgiveness, and acceptance.

THINK ABOUT IT...

1. What are some of the dividing walls that separate Christians into insiders and outsiders?

2. How do comparison, suspicion, and generalization affect relationships?

3. Why does comparison inevitably produce a sense of superiority or inferiority?

4. Describe the transformation in Paul's life from a person who hated Christians and Gentiles to someone who loved them and suffered to take God's love to them.

5. How should Christians talk about politics, especially particular leaders and immigration?

6. In what ways do we think it's acceptable to tolerate people instead of truly loving them? What's wrong with that approach?

7. Which of the suggestions at the end of the chapter do you want to apply? How will you do it? What do you expect to happen?

8. What would it look like if God answered Paul's prayer in your life?

4

UNITY AND DIVERSITY

Ephesians 4:1-16

To serve is beautiful, but only if it is done

with joy and a whole heart and a free mind.

—Pearl S. Buck

When I was a young pastor, I led a church of about a hundred people in Irving, Texas. I was a one-man show. I ran from one responsibility to another. I preached, visited people in the hospital, led committees, met with people who attended for the first time, and I did every other job that needed to be done. I thought I was indispensable, but in reality, I didn't understand my role as the shepherd and equipper of God's people. The harder I worked, the more upset I became over the passivity of others. But to be honest, I didn't give them many opportunities to lead and serve.

Being Superman felt great when people appreciated my tireless efforts, but it stank when I couldn't keep all the balls in the air and people expressed disappointment in me. Actually, the 'S' on my chest didn't stand for 'Superman'—it stood for 'Stupid.' I was running myself ragged and resented people for not appreciating all I was trying to do.

During this season of my life, God led me to a book called *Everyone a Minister* by Oscar Feucht. It transformed my perspective of my role as a pastor. Traditionally, Lutherans have struggled to distinguish between the office of pastoral ministry and what Luther called "the priesthood of all believers." Some church leaders have been afraid that elevating the role of every believer will diminish their positions as pastors. I think that's a false dichotomy. God has called every believer to be completely committed to build his kingdom, and it's the pastor's responsibility to equip each one to be most effective. Both roles are essential. When a pastor tries to be Superman, he robs his people of the joy of seeing God use them, and parishioners remain spiritually flabby because they aren't exercising their talents.

When I read Feucht's book, I made some changes. I shifted my primary role from *doing* the ministry to *training others* to do ministry. I soon realized that the people in our church could fulfill almost all the responsibilities at least as well as I could, and we all enjoyed the process far more when we shared the load. I discovered that people didn't think less of me for empowering and equipping them to be involved in evangelism, discipleship, administration, and other forms of service. I also noticed that none of them assumed they should take my role as the chief equipper of the saints. All those fears disappeared in the joy of seeing people take responsibility and thrive.

Years ago, Gloria Dei was growing, and some pastors of other churches grumbled that our church had "all the gifted people," and they assumed I was cocky about our church's rapid growth. When I learned of their complaints, I went to them and said, "Hey guys, I have no idea why our church is growing. I don't have any more insights than anyone else, and our people aren't any more gifted than yours. It's a mystery of God's grace to me. It's certainly not because of me!"

However, I wasn't content to let it go with that. I told them that the one thing I'd learned was to see myself as the chief equipper and cheerleader of the saints at Gloria Dei. I asked them, "When was the last time you reminded your people that the Spirit of God has empowered them to do the work of the ministry? Affirm that the Holy Spirit has called them and gifted them to change lives. It's your job to help them grasp and live out that great calling. It will be the greatest delight in your people's lives, and it will be your joy to see the thrill in their eyes when God uses them to transform the destinies of the people they know. There is no greater joy in my life than to see our people succeed. They are my joy and crown, and your people's success and drive can thrill you, too."

On the other side of the coin, many people in the pews assume their pastor should do all the work of ministry because "that's what we've hired him to do." They just sit back and watch week after week and year after year. They don't realize that they play a vital role in fulfilling God's purposes and expanding his kingdom.

Two pillars of Martin Luther's Reformation were salvation by grace through faith and the priesthood of all believers. Sadly, 450 years later, we're still trying to put his principles into practice.

TURNING POINT

In the first three chapters of his letter, Paul focuses on God working his grace *into* our lives; now he turns to describe how grace flows *out* to shape our attitudes, choices, and relationships. He wrote, "I therefore, a prisoner for the Lord, urge you to walk in a manner worthy of the calling to which you have been called" (4:1).

Walk worthily. This encouragement isn't just about the outward actions. It also addresses our hidden motives. The Christian life isn't a grind. We don't obey out of guilt or the need to prove ourselves. Instead, we recognize all God has done in our lives—the results of the magnificent grace Paul has described—and we order our lives to please him. In light of God's love and our new identity as his beloved children, it's the only reasonable response to his grace. The Christian life isn't about feeling guilty enough so we feel we have to obey God's harsh laws. It's a response of reciprocal love and loyalty. When we grasp the grace Paul has described in the first three chapters, our hearts sing, "Love so amazing, so divine, demands my life, my soul, my all."[15]

In *The Call*, Os Guinness defines our spiritual calling as "the truth that God calls us to himself so decisively that everything we are, everything we do, and everything we have is invested with a special devotion and dynamism lived out as a response to his summons and service."[16] Paul picks up on these themes and carries them forward. What does it mean to walk in a manner worthy of our calling to live in grace? He wrote, ". . . with all humility and gentleness, with patience, bearing with one another in love, eager to maintain the unity of the Spirit in the bond of peace" (4:2-3). We are so secure in our relationship with Christ that we don't have to jockey for positions of power, and we don't have to cower in fear because we feel so helpless. Radical grace produces true humility. Many people don't understand the essence of biblical humility. They think it implies we roll over at the slightest opposition and let people walk over us. That's not humility—it's weakness and cowardice. Humility isn't thinking less of ourselves; it's thinking of ourselves less. Jesus was the epitome of a humble man. He was gentle and kind, but when the occasion arose, he was as fierce as a lion. Humble people are secure enough to know when to give in and when to push back.

Another product of grace is gentleness. Jesus was on a mission to rescue the world from sin, death, and hell, but he stopped to tenderly

---

15   Isaac Watts, "When I Survey the Wondrous Cross," 1707.
16   Os Guinness, *The Call* (Word Publishing: Nashville, 1998), p. 4.

touch lepers, hold babies in his arms, and speak words of kindness to people who had lost hope. People who are gentle notice the needs of others and take steps to meet those needs without calling attention to themselves. They genuinely care for hurting people, and they go out of their way to help them.

Those who are captivated by God's grace learn to be patient—with their time and with difficult people. They aren't in a huge hurry to accomplish their agenda because they realize God's purposes sometimes overrule their own. And they extend grace to buttheads because they are so grateful God has showered his grace on them. In this way, they "bear with one another in love." They don't insist on being right and getting their way. They are content to let love—not fear or demands—guide their relationships.

Bonds of peace are created when people recognize Christ's sacrifice to break down the dividing walls between them. Then God's love becomes more important than our differences. These bonds are hard won but easily broken. People who are enamored with the grace of God are "eager to maintain" loving, supportive relationships, especially in the face of personal offenses or cultural differences. We can always find plenty of reasons to despise people, but there's one good reason to keep building bridges of love with them. Pick the one.

ONE, ONE, ONE

In every walk of life—careers, school, neighborhoods, friendships, and church—a spirit of competition erodes genuine love. Too often, we spend more time picking out differences than focusing on the threads that can bind us together. It's more exciting to be in conflict, and it's human nature to want to win, but competition slowly but surely ruins relationships.

Our unity with people doesn't just happen. It's the product of a host of factors that provide a firm foundation for strong relationships. Paul makes this very clear:

> There is one body and one Spirit—just as you were called to the one hope that belongs to your call—one Lord, one faith, one baptism, one God and Father of all, who is over all and through all and in all (4:4-6).

In God's family, we come from very different cultures and backgrounds, we are rich and poor, young and old, and of every doctrinal stripe, but in Christ we have an essential unity of heart and spirit. All believers have one Lord, not many versions. We have a faith in God's grace that began in the Garden, was formalized through Abraham, has been refined by the prophets and apostles, and is still the same today in Jesus Christ. Our baptism into God's family is the same for everyone. No one is in God's family unless he's identified with the death, burial, and resurrection of Jesus Christ. We may immerse, sprinkle, or dry clean people, but the meaning is the same. We worship in different ways—some stand and shout while others kneel and pray. But the same God and Father is the Lord of all. He is sovereign over his creation, he knows every hair on our heads, and he will fulfill his eternal purposes in his timing and in his way.

When we think of Christians from other traditions, do we naturally focus on our similarities or differences? Most of us seldom even consider the similarities. We shake our heads because "those people" do it "that way." Take baptism as an example. The Christian church has confessed the meaning of baptism since John baptized Jesus in the Jordan. In Peter's first message, he told people to repent and be baptized. It's always been the way people have identified with Christ, his kingdom, and his family. I was baptized when I was ten days old. Through this sacrament, I became part of the body of Christ and participated in a mysterious, supernatural way in his death and resurrection. At that moment, I was "delivered . . . from the domain of darkness and transferred . . . to the kingdom of his beloved Son" (Colossians 1:13). At that time, God called me his own.

But believers from other traditions hold different views of baptism. Lutherans chide Baptists for re-baptizing while Baptists criticize Lutherans for baptizing infants. In the sixteenth century, people killed each other over this issue! Today, we just look down our noses at those who we consider backward and erring. In the words of Rodney King, "Can't we all get along?" If we stopped long enough to listen, maybe, just maybe, we could learn something from each other. Doesn't infant baptism speak beautifully about grace as God's precious, undeserved gift? If infants are baptized, shouldn't Lutherans remind themselves that this act commits the parents to raise their kids in the nurture and truth of the Christian faith? Those who insist on baptizing adults have a point: How we follow Christ involves decisions—carefully reasoned—to follow him instead of selfish passions. Can't Lutherans appreciate the gravity and joy of these choices for adults? Of course we can, but only if we put down our doctrinaire swords and look into the hearts of those we've suspected of being so wrong. Personally, I believe baptism was God's means of grace to choose, adopt, forgive, and seal me when I was an infant. I hope people—and especially those who disagree with each other—will carefully study each passage about baptism in the Scriptures to understand the true meaning. For example, we need to look at the similarities and differences in the baptism practiced by John the Baptist, Jesus' baptism, believers' baptism in Acts, and the references to it in the rest of the New Testament.

Paul asks us to look for common ground, not bristle at fighting words. When I find that someone is from a different faith tradition, I try to engage the person in conversation to find what's meaningful. I prefer to avoid asking questions like a prosecutor looking for an opening to attack. I try to ask a few innocent questions, and to be sure I'm not misunderstood, I often say, "I appreciate people who come from other traditions. I believe we can all learn from each other's faith in Christ. Would you tell me more about yours?" When people feel honored and understood, the bonds of peace can be built.

GIFTS FROM ABOVE

Our oneness in the body of Christ doesn't make us uniform robots. Instead, God has created a fascinating mosaic of people with the full range of talents, experiences, and passions. Every talent and ability, though, comes from him. We didn't manufacture them. They're his gifts to us. Paul explains the source of our gifts and the intended results:

But grace was given to each one of us according to the measure of Christ's gift. Therefore it says,

> "When he ascended on high he led a host of captives,
>   and he gave gifts to men."

(In saying, "He ascended," what does it mean but that he had also descended into the lower regions, the earth? He who descended is the one who also ascended far above all the heavens, that he might fill all things.) And he gave the apostles, the prophets, the evangelists, the shepherds and teachers, to equip the saints for the work of ministry, for building up the body of Christ (4:7-12).

When Christ ascended back into heaven from the hill outside Jerusalem, his departure detonated a new era for the church. Ten days after he departed, the Holy Spirit came at Pentecost to empower God's people to be the people he wants us to be and do the things he has called us to do. (It's ironic. Christ's ascension was a turning point in history, but it's almost completely overlooked. We send Christmas cards and Easter cards, but I've never received an Ascension card.) When Christ rose into the clouds, he sat at the Father's right hand, but he didn't leave us alone. Paul said he "led a host of captives and he gave gifts to men." When Roman generals conquered foreign armies, they often brought defeated soldiers back to Rome to march behind the triumphant army. Who did Jesus triumph over at the cross? In his letter to the Colossians, Paul explained that on the cross "[Jesus] disarmed the rulers and authorities and put them to open shame, by triumphing over them in him" (Colossians 2:15). Like a conquering Roman general, Jesus paraded defeated demons behind him when he ascended into heaven. And like the general who had gathered the spoils of his conquest and generously shared them with his soldiers and the cheering people, Jesus has given lavish gifts to each of his people, too.

Some people think of grace in very narrow terms. They think we need God's grace so we can be saved, but after that, we're on our own to live the Christian life. Others think of grace operating during their devotional times and in corporate worship, but they seldom think of God the rest of the day. To them, grace is limited to times of prayer and Bible reading. They draw a sharp distinction between the sacred and the secular. Thank God that's not the case, or we'd be in big trouble! For a child of God, grace is comprehensive. He lavishes his grace on us before we believe so he can awaken our hearts to hear the gospel and respond. Without his grace, we'd still be dead in our sins. After we trust in Christ, God's grace continues to empower us, motivate us, and surround us with God's love, protection, and power. This is the work of the Spirit, who enlightens the eyes of our hearts to know God more deeply, corrects us when our motives are impure, and provides power to fulfill God's will. Without the continuing presence of grace in our lives, the Christian life becomes a grind of empty obedience, or we give up because it's just too hard. Grace keeps us going because it keeps us connected to God's loving heart. Spiritual gifts are another aspect of God's grace to us.

In their letters, Paul and Peter include four lists of spiritual gifts (1 Corinthians 12, Romans 12, 1 Peter 4, and Ephesians 4). These often overlap, but they aren't exactly the same. From this, we can conclude that none of the lists is exhaustive. God is far too creative to be limited to a list, and our unique expressions of his power and glory can't be contained in words. The list in Paul's letter to the Ephesians is different from the others. In this letter, Paul doesn't describe talents God has given to each person—instead, he identifies *gifted leaders* he has given to his church. Apostles are those who exercise authority over the church. Prophets foretell God's purposes and forth-tell God's truth. Evangelists have a special ability to connect with unbelievers and explain the gospel in clear, powerful ways. Shepherds and teachers may be a single role, or they might be two separate functions. Shepherds are those who pastor God's flock, and teachers have a talent to make the Scriptures come alive in the hearts of their listeners.[17]

Why did God give these people to the church? Not to stand on a platform and call attention to themselves, but to equip the rest of the

---

17 Some New Testament scholars teach that the first three roles (apostles, prophets, and evangelists) were operative only in the first centuries of the church and ceased after that. Their impact, though, is still felt in the teaching of the New Testament, which describes their ministries.

body of Christ so all believers in the community of faith will be skilled and motivated to honor God in everything they do.

Today, we expect instant results from everything we do. We use microwave ovens and drive-through banking. We have all the information in the world in our pockets and purses on our phones. We get impatient if it takes more than a few seconds for a movie or a YouTube video to load. However, it takes time to equip people to be effective in God's service. Strangely, some pastors today teach that training isn't needed at all, and in fact, it gets in the way of the spontaneous display of the Spirit. That's a foreign concept to Paul and to Jesus. I've never been a good fisherman because no one ever taught me to fish. My father rarely went fishing, and I never developed a desire or talent to catch fish. If I wanted to become an effective fisherman, someone would need to train me. When Jesus called Peter and Andrew, they were already fishermen, but he told them he was going to train them in a different kind of fishing. He said, "Follow me, and I will make you fishers of men" (Matthew 4:19). Jesus didn't say, "You are fishermen." He explained, "I will make you a new breed of fishermen." He took the next three years to retrain their thinking, their expectations, and their behavior so they could become leaders in the church.

Paul's list of gifts in Ephesians is of leaders God gives to the church. The other lists are of specific talents God supernaturally grants to believers whether we are leaders or followers. They range from teaching the Bible to caring for those who are hurting. Our task is to identify and use the gifts God has given us. We can use a three-part grid: opportunity, passion, and effectiveness. When these three are aligned, our hearts sing and we delight in serving God at home, at work, and everywhere we go. Finding this alignment, though, can be a daunting challenge. We may have an open door of opportunity, but we have no desire to do it. Some of us are very skilled at roles, but we don't really enjoy them. We may have a burning passion to serve in a certain way, but all we find are dead ends. There are no magic formulas. We need to keep trying new areas of service until we find one that really fits. That's how we become the masterpiece God created us to be.

Some people need the attention of a pastor or another leader to help them find the right place to serve, but others are entrepreneurs who need only an opportunity and plenty of room to try new things. Good leaders recognize the presence of both kinds of people (and those in between) in their congregations, and they take appropriate steps to equip, direct, and encourage people to find a role that fits. Sometimes, church leaders need to rein in rowdy people, but sometimes they need to let them fly. Great leaders know the difference. Leading creative people is like parenting teenagers. We'd better value their creativity, but we can't let them get too far out of hand. The best organizational chart may not be neat and clean. In his great book, *Built to Last*, Jim Collins advised leaders, "Avoid the tyranny of the 'or,' and embrace the genius of the 'and.' "[18]

From countless conversations over the years, I've found that many people mistakenly compartmentalize their relationship with Christ and assume they need God's gifts and power only when they're doing church work. The rest of the week—the vast majority of their time—is effectively devoid of any sense that this time has eternal value. When are we God's children? All day, every day. When do we represent him? In our homes, our offices, our fields, our schools, and our backyards. When do we need his heart for people and his power to do his will? Every moment of every day. I believe it's the church's responsibility to equip people to be God's hands, feet, and voice when they sit around their dinner tables, when they meet with clients, and when they go to

---

18   Jim Collins and Jerry Porras, *Built to Last* (HarperBusiness, 2004).

ballgames. The principles of integrity, trust, excellence, and honor apply in every situation in life, not just when we're singing or listening to a message, and not just when we're serving inside the walls of the church building. God's kingdom is much bigger than that!

One of the most inspiring compliments I've ever received was from a man who worked at the University of Houston-Clear Lake campus. He told me, "Pastor K, I've learned more about leadership here at our church than I've ever learned at the university." That's the way it should be. We follow the greatest leader the world has ever known. His nature, strategy, and heart should rub off on us and make a difference in how we lead others. I can't impart engineering skills, business strategies, or medical techniques, but I can train people in all these fields to live and lead with compassion, strength, and integrity. The psalmist described the lessons David learned and used when he became king of Israel:

> He chose David his servant
>> and took him from the sheepfolds;
> from following the nursing ewes he brought him
>> to shepherd Jacob his people,
>> Israel his inheritance.
> With upright heart he shepherded them
>> and guided them with his skillful hand (Psalm 78:70-72).

We don't have to be kings or pastors to fulfill our calling. Every believer is called to be God's child and build his kingdom. In our culture, we live in a hierarchy of roles—from the CEO to the janitor. Too often, people in higher orders look down on those who are "beneath them." Luther disabused people of this hierarchy. Every person, no matter how high or humble, plays an important role in the kingdom of God. In fact, all people play the role of Jesus in serving others through their vocation. Luther explained, "All our work in the field, in the garden, in the city, in the home, in struggle, in government—to what does it all amount before God except child's play, by means of which God is pleased to give his gifts in the field, at home, and everywhere? These are the masks of our Lord God, behind which he wants to be hidden and to do all things."[19] Are any vocations so low they don't count? No, even a mother wiping her baby's behind is doing admirable and necessary service—as important to God as a priest consecrating the elements. Cleaning toilets has inherent dignity if it's done for Christ's glory.

When we jockey for position and seek honor, we're acting in a way that is the opposite of Jesus Christ. He stepped out of the glory of heaven to become a man, emptied himself of his privileges, and became the lowest servant—to the point of death on the cross. Our calling isn't about positions of power. It's about character: humility, gentleness, kindness, and love. We can fulfill God's calling in good times and bad, whether we receive honors or if we're overlooked.

If we believe the professional clergy should do all the work of the ministry, the rest of the people are relegated to be observers—or more likely, critics. They sit back on Sunday morning and watch worship instead of joining in. Over lunch, they criticize the finer points of the message and give it a grade. During the rest of the week, they wonder if the pastor and staff are doing enough to help people in need. This way of living is never endorsed in the Scriptures. Yes, clergy play an important role in administering the sacraments and teaching God's word, but every person is a minister (or, if you feel uncomfortable with that term, every person is a servant of Christ), every believer is an

---

19   Martin Luther, *Exposition of Psalm 147*, quoted by Gustaf Wingren, *Luther on Vocation* (Evansville, Indiana: Ballast Press, 1994), p. 138.

ambassador, everyone fills a crucial role in accomplishing Christ's purposes before (and after) he returns.

IF WE'RE EQUIPPED . . .

When people in a congregation identify their gifts and are trained to use them effectively, the body grows wider and deeper. For many of us, diets are good things, but in Christ's body, health means we add a lot more people and each person gets "heavier" with love and maturity. As we serve, teach, speak truth, care, and support each other, wonderful things happen. Paul described it this way:

> . . . until we all attain to the unity of the faith and of the knowledge of the Son of God, to mature manhood, to the measure of the stature of the fullness of Christ, so that we may no longer be children, tossed to and fro by the waves and carried about by every wind of doctrine, by human cunning, by craftiness in deceitful schemes. Rather, speaking the truth in love, we are to grow up in every way into him who is the head, into Christ, from whom the whole body, joined and held together by every joint with which it is equipped, when each part is working properly, makes the body grow so that it builds itself up in love (4:13-16).

The church Paul describes doesn't just sit around and tell each other how wonderful they are. They're bold, strong, and active. They focus their eyes on Christ, not themselves. They stand boldly against false and destructive teaching, just like Jesus corrected the misguided ideas of the Pharisees. They're aware of the enemy's deceptions, and they expose them as lies. In their relationships, they speak the truth, but they don't use truth as a weapon to beat up their opponents. They genuinely love people, so they gently correct them when they need it. Paul then returns to the metaphor of a body and says that when each part functions properly, the body grows. The implication is that when any individual part fails to work like it's supposed to, the body suffers. Every person listening to Paul's letter instinctively understands this truth. When a person has an ingrown toenail, the tiny problem causes his whole life to be disrupted. When our bodies are doing well, we don't think about our elbows, knees, or the bones in our ears that enable us to hear. But when any part of us hurts, every part of us is adversely affected.

Over the years, I've seen the eyes of countless people light up when they grasped the concept that God has called and equipped them to be ministers and servants. A good friend of mine attended church his whole life, but he was just going through the motions. I'm not sure why he came week after week. Maybe it was habit, or maybe he liked the coffee. When he heard Paul's teaching that every believer is called, every believer is a masterpiece of grace, and every believer plays a vital role in God's kingdom, it was like someone lit a fire in his soul. He was suddenly energized, and he had new, innovative ideas about how to touch people's lives. He told me, "John, I don't know why I didn't get it before, but I get it now. I want my life to count. God has given me every blessing so I can pour his love, strength, and peace into others. It's the happiest time of my life!" He had a new passion for Jesus Christ and a new passion to serve him, and his passion has only intensified since then.

GRACE IN ACTION

For years, seminaries taught that getting people into worship, Bible study, and prayer would change their lives so they'd want to serve. That may have been true for generations, but the script has flipped today, at least among young people. In our day, the "front door" of a life of faith consists of opportunities to serve. When they get involved in caring for the homeless, the helpless, single moms, abuse victims, and refugees from war-torn foreign lands, they become sensitized to the message of the gospel. Acts of service open their hearts to the truth about Jesus.

A small group of five couples of twenty-somethings had been meeting together for several years. They enjoyed talking about the Scriptures, eating dinner and hanging out, but there wasn't a sense of purpose in their group. One day, a guy in the group told them about a man who lived down the street. He had lost his job and his family had left him. "He needs some help," he explained. "Maybe we can do something." They pitched in to provide him some immediate relief of groceries, and one of them offered to drive him to a job interview. Their tangible assistance was valuable, but it paled in comparison to the emotional and spiritual support they gave him. He got the job and his family returned. The neighbor and his wife joined the group, and they told them, "You gave us our lives back. We don't know how to thank you." This group now has finely tuned antennae to pick up needs in their community. Sometimes, they provide all the help that's needed; often, they point people to resources in the community. Either way, everybody wins. They've come alive.

A young woman came to our church and discovered her new identity as a gifted, called child of God. The Lord gave her a desire to start tutoring disadvantaged kids in reading and math. She started with a child or two, and the floodgates opened. She came to me and asked if the church would help to sponsor her ministry. I was thrilled to help her in any way I could. She gathered a team of talented, compassionate people around her and they made a difference in hundreds of young lives. She and her team found meaning and purpose as they poured themselves into the lives of others.

Bold acts to care for the helpless can be both a front door and the ultimate result of a vibrant faith. In 2005, Hurricane Katrina barreled into the Gulf of Mexico and headed north. For several days, those who lived all along the coast from Texas to Florida wondered where this monster would come ashore. Finally, it took aim at New Orleans. The first reports were encouraging. The damage from the wind and storm surge wasn't as bad as the experts predicted. A few hours later, however, the dikes collapsed and much of the city was under several feet of water. The national news networks carried continuous coverage of the devastation and the fight for life. In the next few days, tens of thousands of displaced people needed to find new homes.

I got a call from the Red Cross. The official asked if our church would be an official shelter for those who were fleeing New Orleans. We scheduled a meeting for 9:30 the next morning. By noon, people were knocking on our door asking for help. We called our people and asked them to open their homes. We didn't screen the people arriving from Louisiana, so we could give our people no assurances they were safe or clean. The people of Gloria Dei were magnificent. They opened their hearts and their doors. That night and for the next week or so, our people housed, clothed, and fed almost 200 people who had nowhere to go.

I was so proud of our people. I was even more gratified weeks later when people in the community reflected on all that happened and told me, "Pastor, we knew Gloria Dei would come through for those people. That's who you are." Our people were masterpieces of God's grace. They lived out their calling to give, serve, and care for others. That's how Christ lived, and that's how our people showed up in the days after Katrina.

The apostle Paul would have agreed with Mark Twain when he said, "The two most important days of your life are the day you are born and the day you find out why."

THINK ABOUT IT...

1. What do you think it means for us to "walk in a manner worthy of the calling to which we've been called"?

2. What are some reasons we may gravitate to identify roles we can play instead of focusing on developing and living out Christ's character?

3. What is the impact of a spirit of competition on the unity in the body of Christ? How do you see it in conversations and attitudes? What can you do about it when you find it in yourself?

4. Have you found the best fit for you and your gifts? How would you describe the blend of your opportunity, passion, and effectiveness in serving God?

5. What does it mean to "speak the truth in love"? Who do you know who consistently relates to people this way? What are the results? What are the risks?

6. For you, is serving others a front door to a richer, more vibrant faith, or is it the result of spiritual disciplines lived for a long time? Explain your answer.

7. What would a group of believers look like if they truly lived out the truths of this part of Paul's letter? Is it attractive to you? Why or why not?

5

LEARNING CHRIST

Ephesians 4:17–5:21

If Christ lives in us, controlling our personalities,

we will leave glorious marks on the lives we touch.

Not because of our lovely characters, but because of his.

—Eugenia Price

A young couple, Sarah and James, came to me and asked me to marry them. I told them I'd be delighted, and I wanted to get to know them before the wedding. As we talked, I asked some simple questions that elicited awkward looks. I asked them where they were living, and they said they were living together. Sarah quickly explained that the apartment where she'd been living had been burglarized, and she didn't feel safe there any more. James had offered for her to stay in his home. They were already committed to getting married, so it seemed natural for them to live together.

In the conversation, both of them expressed faith in Jesus Christ. They wanted their marriage to be founded on God's grace. I was pleased but perplexed. I asked, "Are you having sex?"

James answered, "No, Pastor. We're not. We stay in separate rooms."

Sarah looked a bit sheepish, but she nodded. I had to take their word for it. Still, I asked, "Do you think living together before marriage reflects well on Christ? Do you think it tells others the right message about his will and his ways?"

When people ask me for help to determine a direction about any important decision in their lives, I almost always say, "There are always several options to consider. What is in line with the will and the mind of Christ?" In Paul's letter to the Ephesians, he intuitively asks this question and provides a clear, powerful framework for the answers. He addresses how people think and the way spiritual change happens. Then he provides a number of concrete examples of good and godly choices. Finally, he reminds his readers (including us) that we're not alone. God has given us the ultimate source of wisdom and power to do his will. Let's look at each of these concepts. They provide handles and hope for living a truly *Christian* life.

THINK!

Some of us are highly reflective, but many respond emotionally and spontaneously to the circumstances of life. At a point in my career when I felt betrayed and attacked by those I trusted, I developed a deep sense of resentment. I was deeply upset. How could they do this to me? Initial anger remained unresolved, so it soon festered into full-blown bitterness. I got two things from these feelings: a sense of identity as the one who was wronged and the adrenaline rush of despising those who had hurt me. I've heard people say that bitterness is a poison that only affects the inside of the bottle. The longer I held on to the hurt, anger, and resentment, the more miserable I became. I realized I couldn't feel my way out of this predicament—the pain was too strong, and the desire for revenge was too delicious. I had to start from scratch. I had to learn how to think biblically about the people and the situation.

Throughout the Bible, the writers invite us to think, ponder, consider, reason, reflect, and remember. God gave Abraham repeated promises so he wouldn't forget. God led Moses and the former Egyptian slaves with pillars of smoke and fire, and the Lord gave them an ark, tablets of stone, a rod, sacrifices, and ceremonies to remind them of the "furious opposites" of his unapproachable majesty and his intimate tenderness. When the children of Israel crossed the Jordan, God told them to erect stone piles in the river as monuments to his faithfulness. In Paul's letters, he often refers back to historical events and previously explained truths to refresh the memories of his readers. In Romans, after he has described the wonder of the gospel of grace in the fullest details, he asks, "What then shall we say to these things?" (Romans 8:31) He's inviting us to apply all he has taught before. And a few chapters later, he again encourages his readers to reflect on God's truth so they can live it out. He wrote, "I appeal to you therefore, brothers, by the mercies of God [which he had described in the first eleven chapters], to present your bodies a living sacrifice, holy and acceptable to God, which is your spiritual worship" (Romans 12:1). Again and again, the biblical authors root our current choices of loyalty in the history of God's love. Today, we have the Scriptures, worship, the sacraments, and spiritual disciplines to keep our minds riveted on God's glory and goodness.

The Christian faith is more than mental (it's also volitional, emotional, and relational), but responding to God in every situation necessitates rigorous mental involvement. In our culture, our minds are flooded with messages and images, and we seldom stop to consider the source. Paul says we can be deceived in many different ways. Sinful, selfish human nature tries to justify our destructive behavior by telling us, "Everybody's doing it. No problem!" Satan whispers in our ears that we deserve better than we're getting, but we don't notice because he disguises his voice to sound like ours. And the culture screams at us all day, every day. The constant barrage of advertising tells us we should be thinner, richer, and more popular, and we'll fulfill these dreams if we buy this product or that service. In , Jacques Ellul explained that advertising creates an expectation for an ideal life of ease, plenty, and fun. Many people pursue this ideal at the expense of real values, relationships, and purpose in life.[20] In a CNN article, "The Power of Advertising," Monita Rajpal observed,

> Everywhere we go, everywhere we look, we are inundated with messages. We don't even have to think for ourselves. All we have to do is sit on our comfy couch and be told how to live our lives. From how to look, what to wear, what to eat, what our homes should look like, how to meet people, what to drive, practically every facet of our lives is taken care of. That is the power of advertising. . . . In this age of multiple mediums, advertising is everywhere—whether it's a pop-up campaign with people dancing at the train station (T-Mobile) that serves a multitude of platforms from television to the web, or a home-video-type commercial that is posted on You-Tube. We may not have to think for ourselves as much but we do have to be more discriminating to decipher what is credible and what isn't. Bottom line though, advertising is a part of our existence. The good news is we're the ones with the power to choose.[21]

Ephesus in the first century wasn't much different from our society and pressures today. Human nature, the enemy's schemes, and the

---

20   Cited at jan.ucc.nau.edu/~jsa3/hum355/readings/ellul.htm.
21   "The Power of Advertising," Monita Rajpal, CNN, cited on www.cnn.com/2010/WORLD/europe/09/22/power.of.advertising/index.html

lure of more possessions, power, and pleasure were a struggle for them as much as they are for us. Into this confusing matrix of messages, Paul almost yells, "Wake up! Look at what's going on in your head, and learn to think with the mind of Christ." He wrote:

> Now this I say and testify in the Lord, that you must no longer walk as the Gentiles do, in the futility of their minds. They are darkened in their understanding, alienated from the life of God because of the ignorance that is in them, due to their hardness of heart. They have become callous and have given themselves up to sensuality, greedy to practice every kind of impurity (4:17-19).

Change necessarily involves what happens between our ears. Too often, we get frustrated by a lack of spiritual growth, but we don't do the hard work of identifying the mental dams and dikes that prevent the flow of the Spirit. We're all still in process. Mature believers still wrestle with deceptions and temptations, but they're quicker to recognize them and replace them. All of us need to stay on our toes. Paul said that apart from Christ, our thoughts are futile and our understanding is darkened. People who reject Christ and his ways often assume they're the brightest and most enlightened people in the world. They've walked away from the historical facts of the incarnation, cross, and resurrection as fables, but they claim Christ's moral teaching gives us a good example of how to live. That's baloney. Christ taught clearly about himself as the Savior, the eternal "I Am," the light, the bread, and the living water. It's foolish and inconsistent to cling to part of his teaching and reject the rest. He hasn't left that option open to us.

To the extent people soak their minds in false statements and wrong assumptions—about God, about themselves, and about the way life works—they live in ignorance, and they become hardened in their foolish assumptions. Before long, they can't tell the difference between right and wrong. Sin becomes the subject of entertainment, and righteousness is ridiculed. Without God's moral compass and his Spirit's power and love, people are left with this philosophy: "If it feels good, do it." We see the destructive results of that perspective every day.

"But wait," some would argue, "aren't you being too dramatic? Surely wrong thinking doesn't cause that much harm. It's not like there's blood or anything." In his book, *People of the Lie*, Scott Peck addressed the insidious nature of evil. He wrote,

> When I say that evil has to do with killing, I do not mean to restrict myself to corporeal murder. Evil is that which kills spirit. There are various essential attributes of life—particularly human life—such as sentience, mobility, awareness, growth, autonomy, will. It is possible to kill or attempt to kill one of these attributes without actually destroying the body. Thus we may 'break' a horse or even a child without harming a hair on its head. . . . Evil then, for the moment, is the force, residing either inside or outside of human beings, that seeks to kill life or liveliness. And goodness is its opposite. Goodness is that which promotes life and liveliness.[22]

Is our situation hopeless? With all the distractions, can we ever think properly so we can experience true life and liveliness? Paul gives us the solution.

CHANGING CLOTHES

Paul uses the eraser word again: "But that is not the way you learned Christ" (4:20). He uses the metaphor of changing clothes

---

22   M. Scott Peck, *People of the Lie* (Touchstone, 1998), p. 43.

to demonstrate the choices of a transformed heart. When I change clothes, I don't try to put clean clothes over the dirty ones. (If I did, Elaine would get pretty upset with me.) I first recognize that my clothes are dirty and something has to change. Recognizing evil in others is hard; recognizing it in ourselves is much more difficult. The human heart runs on rationalization like a plane flies on jet fuel. When we look back at the first chapters of the Bible, God gave Adam and Eve a directive and a choice: Don't eat from the tree of the knowledge of good and evil. When they sinned, Adam blamed Eve, and then he blamed God. It takes courage to take an honest look at our lives and call sin by its name. Two millennia ago, Jesus came "full of grace and truth"—not with empty, superficial sweetness or harsh condemnation. He looked evil in the face and died to forgive it.

Paul described the process:

> But that is not the way you learned Christ!—assuming that you have heard about him and were taught in him, as the truth is in Jesus, to put off your old self, which belongs to your former manner of life and is corrupt through deceitful desires, and to be renewed in the spirit of your minds, and to put on the new self, created after the likeness of God in true righteousness and holiness (4:20-24).

The "old self" is our fallen, flawed human nature—selfishness, giving in to temptation, greed, bitterness, being judgmental, arrogance, cowardice, and all other patterns of sin—that won't vanish from our experience until we meet Jesus face to face. Some Christians are confused about the continued reality of sin in their lives. Martin Luther famously said our condition is *simul iustus et peccator*, simultaneously saint and sinner. That's certainly true in my own life, and every reflective Christian understands Luther's description. Our sinful natures aren't improving; they never give up! That's why we keep fighting, wrestling, and trusting in God's grace and power throughout our lives.

Dirty clothes don't just fall off me. I have to unbutton, unzip, and take off each part individually. That's the first part of repentance. I make a choice to say "No" to the sinful habits I've had, realize the destruction they've caused me and those I love, and lay them aside. But that's not the end of the process. Paul says we need to have our minds renewed so we learn to value what God values and see life through the lens of faith in Christ. This process takes a lifetime, and I suspect it may not end even there. As we spend time with God in the new heaven and new earth, we'll keep learning more about the wonder of his greatness and grace.

The spiritual disciplines give us a "mind transplant." Bible reading, prayer, fellowship, service, confession, and the Eucharist are some of the means by which God gives us grace to dig deeper into the thoughts and heart of Christ. Gradually, our minds are renewed and we increasingly think God's thoughts about our circumstances and relationships. Our thinking has been futile, but now it is shaped by the powerful truth of the Scriptures and the tender love of God. During this process, we make thousands of choices to "put on the new self." What does that mean? It means we become a little more like Jesus. We stop believing riches, popularity, and control will fill the hole in our hearts. We turn to Christ for wisdom, love, and power. With his help, we love the unlovely, bless the poor, weep with those who weep, and rejoice with those who rejoice. In every situation, we ask, "What does Jesus want to do in me and through me? What is my natural inclination, and what is the choice that honors him?" In reference to the significance of our baptism, Luther said that every day we should "repent and drown the old Adam." That's what Paul was talking about in his letter to the Ephesians.

Accounts in the first centuries of the church record instances when believers were stripped of their old clothes and entered baptism completely naked. When they came out of the water, they were given new white robes to wear. This vividly symbolized the removal of sin and the believer being clothed with Christ's righteousness in his new nature. In the fourth century, John Chrysostom summarized the right response to God: "In the heart, contrition; in the mouth, confession; in the work, entire humility."[23]

We "learn Christ" when we despair about the depravity of our hearts. We confess our emptiness and powerlessness—which results in wearing masks of superiority or wallowing in feelings of guilt—we fill our minds with truth and grace, and we make new choices that reflect our new calling as God's children and masterpieces. This transformation takes time. The illustrations in the Scriptures are usually agrarian, not mechanical . . . and they certainly aren't electronic! Human beings don't change at the speed of light. We change and grow like plants that develop from careful tending over time.

LET'S GET PRACTICAL

As a good pastor, Paul anticipates his readers' questions. He doesn't want anyone to be confused about how to apply the power and principles of grace, so he gives five specific applications about how we lay sin aside and put on a Christ-honoring lifestyle.

Lies and truth

First, Paul goes back to the topic of deception and honesty. He wrote, "Therefore, having put away falsehood, let each one of you

---

23 John Chrysostom, cited in "The Apology of the Augsburg Confession," www.immanuelmankato.org/libmaterial/apology/part17.html

speak the truth with his neighbor, for we are members one of another"
(4:25). In our culture, telling lies is a kind of game. People see how
much they can get away with before they get caught, and even then,
they may keep telling lies to get out of the consequences. This isn't true
only of junior high kids. Out of fear or greed, many people exaggerate
the truth to look a little better or make others appear a little worse.
We tell half-truths if they get us out of trouble, and we manipulate the
facts to get what we want. We lie to our enemies, our competitors, our
friends, our spouses, and our children—and we lie to ourselves when
we insist, "It doesn't hurt anybody."

Paul doesn't say, "Lie a little less," or "Don't be quite so obvious."
He says, "Put lying away from you. Flush it, incinerate it, and get rid
of it." That's the "putting off" part. Then, Paul tells us to "put on"
speaking the truth. Why? Because we're members of the same body.
When one part of a person's body lies to another, all kinds of problems
arise. Spasms, disorders, and auto-immune diseases are just a few of
the results. Isn't that what we see in the body of Christ when we lie to
each other?

Telling the truth always comes with inherent risks. It may make us
look bad because we've done something wrong, or it may offend others
because we "out" them about something they've done. The risks can
be high, but the risks of lying and avoiding the truth are even steeper.

Anger and . . . anger

No, that's not a typo. Many Christians believe all anger is sin,
so they redefine it in their own lives. They claim they're *frustrated* or
upset, but they can't bring themselves to be honest about the reality
of their anger. Actually, anger is a normal human response to threat
or loss. There's nothing inherently wrong with the feeling of anger.
In fact, there's something very wrong if we *aren't* angry at injustice or

abuse. It's sin to be passive and numb when we see someone being victimized—including ourselves. Paul instructed, "Be angry and do not sin; do not let the sun go down on your anger, and give no opportunity to the devil" (4:26-27).

Anger at injustice is obligatory, not optional—and certainly not sinful. However, anger festers into resentment and the thirst for revenge when we don't resolve it quickly. It's a bomb waiting to go off, so we need to defuse it soon. Paul's guideline is to deal with it within the day the event happened. When Elaine and I got married, a good friend gave me some advice. She said, "John, don't go to bed mad at Elaine, or you'll wake up mad at her. Don't let that happen!" Paul directs us to address the offense or misunderstanding and seek resolution before we go to sleep. If we wait too long, Satan plants the seed of bitterness, and then it becomes a much bigger deal.

Stealing and working

There are many kinds of theft. Burglary may be the first thing we think about, but other forms are "cooking the books," wasting time at work, taking up others' time, and intentionally slowing down production. People who break in and steal stuff run when someone sees them, but when these others are caught, they make excuses like, "Hey, everybody's doing it" or "The boss doesn't care."

Paul wrote, "Let the thief no longer steal, but rather let him labor, doing honest work with his own hands, so that he may have something to share with anyone in need" (4:28). Laziness and greed prompt stealing, and essentially, they are both forms of stealing from others. Paul says to lay those aside and replace them with the opposites: hard work and generosity. Will we be leeches sucking people dry, or will we be sources of blessing for everyone around us? That's our choice.

Foul-mouthed or encouraging

There's a direct line between our hearts and our mouths. The Pharisees were fierce in their criticism of Jesus, but they felt they were doing God's will by blasting him. Jesus responded, "You brood of vipers! How can you speak good, when you are evil? For out of the abundance of the heart the mouth speaks" (Matthew 12:34). Paul picked up this connection in his next application. Our words, he explained, can kill or cure: "Let no corrupting talk come out of your mouths, but only such as is good for building up, as fits the occasion, that it may give grace to those who hear. And do not grieve the Holy Spirit of God, by whom you were sealed for the day of redemption" (4:29-30).

If we passed every word through the grid of grace, many of our homes would be much quieter! Some of us delight in verbal battles. We use words like clubs and swords to bludgeon and cut those we claim to love. If we use our words to control or condemn, we need to stop it. But that's not enough. Nature abhors a vacuum. We need to fill the void with the grace and truth of Jesus Christ. A friend observed that we are all like huge buckets filled with something. When we're jostled by life's difficulties and stresses, whatever is in our buckets spills out. What spills out of your mouth and mine when we're jostled today? If it's resentment, self-pity, blame, denial, or anything like that, we need to go back to the source, put off the old, let God renew our minds, and put on the new self full of love, peace, and joy.

The benchmark of every conversation should be: "How can I give grace to this person?" That doesn't mean we only say happy, pleasant things. We give grace to someone who is ruining his life by pointing out the error, inviting repentance, and assuring the person of God's (and our) forgiveness.

It's interesting that Paul injects a statement at this point in his list of applications: "And do not grieve the Holy Spirit of God." The

Spirit isn't an "it." He is a divine person with emotions. We delight him or grieve him by our responses. In Paul's description of a Christ-honoring lifestyle, he implies that the words we say to one another affect the Holy Spirit's emotions. Like all our choices, our communication with one another thrills him or makes him very sad.

Bitterness and forgiveness

We live in a fallen world with fallen people. The church doesn't make us immune from hurts and bitterness. Actually, I think being Christians raises our expectations in relationships and makes us more vulnerable to hurts and disappointments (but we may need to save that for another book someday). Rifts between people are the most painful, damaging, and life-sucking things that happen to us. I've known people whose lives have been eaten away by decades of bitterness, self-pity, and thoughts of revenge.

Some people try to deal with deep hurts by denying the wound even exists. Others soak up all the blame because it's too painful to have an honest conversation with the one who hurt them. Still others try to tell themselves the offender didn't really mean it or it wasn't that bad after all. None of these strategies works. We have to be honest about the offense and take it to the cross. Otherwise, the hurt boils in our souls and ruins every aspect of our lives. Paul wrote, "Let all bitterness and wrath and anger and clamor and slander be put away from you, along with all malice. Be kind to one another, tenderhearted, forgiving one another, as God in Christ forgave you" (4:31-32).

Paul doesn't want to leave any variety of resentment out of his list! He includes outbursts and slow simmers, ferocious confrontations and sly backstabbing. It's human nature to try to punish people who have hurt us, but Jesus offers a very different way. He absorbed our debt and set us free. When we forgive, we don't excuse or minimize the hurt, but we also don't harbor the desire for revenge. We absorb the debt and let the person go free. Author and pastor Lewis Smedes offered this insight: "Vengeance is having a videotape planted in your soul that cannot be turned off. It plays the painful scene over and over again inside your mind. . . . And each time it plays you feel the clap of pain again. . . . Forgiving turns off the videotape of pained memory. Forgiving sets you free."[24]

When we bravely absorb the debt incurred by an offense, we suspend our desire for revenge. Instead of returning evil for evil, we hope for good in the person's life. But what about justice? Some of us refuse to forgive because it seems so unfair to let the offender off the hook. In his letter to the Romans, Paul explains that when we forgive, we take people off our hook and put them on God's. He wrote, "Beloved, never avenge yourselves, but leave it to the wrath of God, for it is written, 'Vengeance is mine, I will repay, says the Lord'" (Romans 12:19). We can forgive because God has forgiven us first and because we have the assurance that God will be just with the offender. Can we trust him with that? If not, we'll insist on continuing to seek revenge (overtly or covertly). If we trust God, we forgive the offense, grieve the hurt, wish the person well, and see if there is hope for reconciliation.

It's essential to separate forgiveness from reconciliation. One does not necessarily lead to the other. If we forgive and the person repents, trust can begin to be rebuilt. If the person refuses to admit his offense—or worse, blames us for the problem—we still forgive, but we're foolish to trust. Trust must be earned . . . slowly, carefully, and wisely. Forgiveness, then, is our unilateral commitment to obey God about the hurt we've experienced, but reconciliation requires both parties to take steps toward each other.

---

24 Lewis Smedes, *Quiet Times for Couples* (Harvest House Publishers: Eugene, Oregon, 1990), p. 91.

These five examples of a changed life show how we can apply the principles outlined earlier in the chapter. Paul didn't want his instructions to stay on the shelf. If they matter at all, they matter in every relationship and every endeavor. These five represent all the possibilities of honesty, repentance, new ways of thinking, and establishing good and godly habits.

Whose Partner?

Paul wasn't naïve about the challenges his readers faced in the first century in Ephesus, and we face the same dilemmas today. People are made for relationships. We desperately need them, and we can't thrive without them. In junior high and high school, finding the right peer group is one of the biggest tasks in life. Throughout our lives, we face similar choices: Whose friend and partner will we be? We have dozens of choices, but one is most important. We have to choose—every day and sometimes every minute of the day—if we're going to be friends with God or friends with the forces of darkness. That's where Paul goes now in his letter.

First, he reminds us of God's good intentions and our reasonable response: "Therefore be imitators of God, as beloved children. And walk in love, as Christ loved us and gave himself up for us, a fragrant offering and sacrifice to God" (5:1-2). We aren't God's business clients who negotiate deals with him. We aren't puppets who have no say in our lives. We aren't prisoners who remain condemned in front of him. We are his beloved children who delight in his love and are thrilled to join him in accomplishing his purposes. Have you seen how kids who are thoroughly convinced of their parents' love follow their example? Little children try to wear their parents' clothes and walk like them. Adult children who have been loved all their lives usually take on the values of their parents and long to honor them in all they do. If you've had parents who loved you like that, call or send a note today to thank them. If you haven't had earthly parents who were thrilled to call you their own, know you have a heavenly Father who is delighted with you.

How much does God love us? We measure love by how much it gives, and Jesus gave it all. On the cross, he absorbed the sins of the world, suffered the excruciating pain of being separated from the Father so he could pay the price for us. His offering, though, wasn't out of guilt or compulsion. His death was a "fragrant offering," the kind given in the temple to celebrate an important occasion. The supreme act of sacrifice was also the supreme act of delighted love. That's the one we follow. That's the one we imitate.

Paul then describes the choice we make to pick God over the alluring temptations of the world. He wrote,

> But sexual immorality and all impurity or covetousness must not even be named among you, as is proper among saints. Let there be no filthiness nor foolish talk nor crude joking, which are out of place, but instead let there be thanksgiving. For you may be sure of this, that everyone who is sexually immoral or impure, or who is covetous (that is, an idolater), has no inheritance in the kingdom of Christ and God. Let no one deceive you with empty words, for because of these things the wrath of God comes upon the sons of disobedience. Therefore do not become partners with them; for at one time you were darkness, but now you are light in the Lord. Walk as children of light (for the fruit of light is found in all that is good and right and true), and try to discern what is pleasing to the Lord. Take no part in the unfruitful works of darkness, but instead expose them. For it is shameful even to speak of the things that they do in secret. But when anything is exposed by the

light, it becomes visible, for anything that becomes visible is light. Therefore it says,

"Awake, O sleeper,
and arise from the dead,
and Christ will shine on you" (5:3-14).

Every day, we have many choices to partner with darkness or light. We make decisions about our sexuality, greed, language, and jokes. At every moment, we face a fork in the road: Will we ally ourselves with God and his kingdom or with the forces of darkness? Ignoring the darkness isn't enough. Paul says we need to go on the offensive and expose evil and sin around us. That doesn't give us a license to blast people into oblivion because they're sinning. Again, we look to Christ. He waded into relationships with all kinds of people, including the down-and-outers and the up-and-comers. No one was off limits to his grace, but he spoke the hard truth to those who resisted his love—not to harm them, but to invite them to come near.

Paul tells us to wake up! Many people come to church or attend classes and groups, but they're spiritual zombies. Their bodies are moving but their souls are asleep! I'm not trying to be cruel. That's the warning Paul gave to the Ephesians. Would he give us a different one today? I don't think so. It's easy to go through the motions without being gripped by grace. Don't let that happen to you. (And don't let it happen to me!) It's easy to drift away. In one of his letters to the Corinthians, Paul gave a similar warning: "But I am afraid that as the serpent deceived Eve by his cunning, your thoughts will be led astray from a sincere and pure devotion to Christ" (2 Corinthians 11:3). If we're not careful, sin becomes amusing, lust becomes normal, and darkness crowds out God's light. In his New Testament commentary,

Oscar Cullmann observed that Paul expected the church's purity and holiness to stand in stark contrast to the Roman world, which was captivated by sex, power, and greed. History shows that those Christians got the message and were beacons of light to their world. Within 200 years, the number of Christians grew from a handful to the dominant force in the empire. What kind of influence do Christians have on our culture today? Are we the same kind of light and salt, or have we just blended in?

Paul's stern admonitions in this section of his letter aren't out of place. As a wise, loving pastor, he knows we need these warnings. God's law is a *mirror* to show us our sin, a *curb* to keep our selfish desires in check, and a *guide* to direct our choices. The law doesn't negate God's grace. The directives and demands for holiness point us again and again to God's love, grace, power, and purpose. If we want to walk with God and be his partners, we do it on his terms, not ours. He is the awesome Alpha and Omega. We are his grateful, loyal children.

One of the misapplications of this section of the letter is to use the five examples and the list of sins in the following paragraph as a checklist to measure other people's holiness (or lack of it). "Look at her," we may say aloud or silently. But that's not why Paul wrote these words. We need to first take the log out of our own eye before we try to help others with the specks in theirs. If we use a checklist, we need to use it on ourselves, and give others as much grace as we desperately need.

THE ULTIMATE RESOURCE

We aren't alone as we try to learn Christ. God has put his Spirit in us to give us the wisdom and strength we need. Today, some Christians complain that God's will is too distant or too complicated. Certainly, some of the finer points of guidance can be a challenge, but we need to put the big, obvious pieces of the puzzle into place first. Do we know how God wants us to relate to him? It's crystal clear that he wants us to love him above all else. How should we treat others? God has told us to love without hypocrisy and love them with the same intention and devotion that we care for our own needs. Is it okay to lie, steal, or commit adultery? For a moral compass, we can start with the Ten Commandments. Many Christians attend church for decades but can't list these ancient and honored commands from the mouth of God. Paul tells us to walk in wisdom. We're really dumb to have all the love and power of the Spirit of God at our fingertips and live as if we were paupers. Paul previously told us that the Spirit has been given to us as a guarantee of the future inheritance in the new heaven and new earth, and he reminded us that the Spirit that lives inside us is the same power that raised Jesus from the dead.

Paul explained,

> Look carefully then how you walk, not as unwise but as wise, making the best use of the time, because the days are evil. Therefore do not be foolish, but understand what the will of the Lord is. And do not get drunk with wine, for that is debauchery, but be filled with the Spirit, addressing one another in psalms and hymns and spiritual songs, singing and making melody to the Lord with your heart, giving thanks always and for everything to God the Father in the name of our Lord Jesus Christ, submitting to one another out of reverence for Christ (5:15-21).

What does it mean to "be filled with the Spirit"? It simply means to be filled and overflowing with Jesus. The Holy Spirit isn't a magic genie to give us what we want, and he's not an electric current we can turn on and off. Through him, we have a relationship with God. Increasingly, we're amazed at the wondrous fact that God has adopted us as his own. As we depend on him, he produces in us the traits of a beloved child: gratitude, love, joy, and humility.

It's interesting that Paul uses wine and drunkenness to compare and contrast the work of the Spirit. Too much wine controls our lives, deadening our senses and warping our judgment, but when the Spirit of God fills us and keeps filling us, it has the opposite effect—we love God, love others, and walk in wisdom and joy.

Deep in our hearts, every true Christian longs to live in a way that pleases God. As we strive to know him and honor him, the Spirit affirms the glorious fact that we are God's children, and he shows us areas that aren't honoring him. When we read this section of Paul's letter, we realize we aren't "holy as he is holy." We are flawed, fallen, and faulty. Instead of groveling in self-pity or blaming others, the right response is to pray, confess our sins, and let the cleansing flood of God's grace wash over us again. When our hearts are filled with Christ, we enjoy a security and satisfaction that can't be described in words. While Jesus was talking to the woman at the well and helping her experience his grace, his disciples went to town to get something to eat. When they came back and offered lunch to Jesus, he told them, "I have food to eat that you do not know about" (John 4:32). There's no higher or deeper satisfaction in my life than knowing I've pleased the Father and honored the Son by following the Spirit's lead. This sense of pervasive joy isn't relegated to worship on Sunday morning. Every second of every day, we have choices to please the one who rescued us, bought us, and adopted us. Every moment is a God moment.

THINK ABOUT THIS...

1. How can we tell the impact of a person's thoughts on his behavior? What are the signs of mental input and output?

2. In what way does sin deaden our hearts? What are some results of this happening to a person (relationally, volitionally, emotionally, spiritually, etc)?

3. Describe in your own words Paul's metaphor of changing clothes.

4. Which of the spiritual disciplines have been most helpful in renewing your mind? Which ones do you need to brush up on? How will they help?

5. Look at the five examples Paul gives of putting off and putting on.
    Which one do you need to apply? How will you do it?

6. Was your relationship with your parents a good example of how a
    loved child imitates his parents? Explain your answer. No matter
    how good or bad it was, what is your motivation to imitate our
    heavenly Father now?

7. Do you agree with Paul and me that many Christians are asleep?
    What does it take to wake us up?

8. What does it mean to be filled with the Spirit? In what way is it
    an event? In what way is it a process? How would you describe the
    results God produces in us when his Spirit fills us?

6

CHANGED CONNECTIONS

Ephesians 5:22-6:9

The family is our refuge and springboard; nourished on it, we can

advance to new horizons. In every conceivable manner, the family is

the link to our past, the bridge to our future.

—Alex Haley

In many ways, we instinctively measure our lives by the quality of our relationships. Our connections with those closest to us give us the highest joys, but they also cause our deepest hurts. If the magnificent love of Christ makes any difference at all in our lives, it will transform our most important relationships: marriage, parenting, and work.

For pastors, it's a time-tested principle that many of the smiles they see in the pews on Sunday during worship have been recently painted on. One Sunday when I was speaking on this passage in Paul's letter, I made the observation that only a few minutes earlier in their homes and cars, spouses were bickering, children were complaining, and most people were fussing about something. But as soon as the car doors opened in the parking lot, everybody looked like a scene from *Ozzie and Harriet* . . . not *The Simpsons*!

When we experience tension and disappointment in our homes and at work, our minds easily drift to compare and idealize. We think, *If I just had a husband like hers*, or *I'd be happy if my boss treated me like that,* or *No wonder that couple is happy—they have perfect kids.* I've wrestled with these thoughts, and I've had to come to grips with the reality that the gospel is meant to work in the lives of deeply flawed people, not perfect ones. Idealizing marriage, parenting, and work eventually leads to deep discouragement—and often, it doesn't take long. In his letter, Paul doesn't have any delusions that these relationships will be easy, but he puts them in the context of God's staggering love.

MANAGING OR LOVING

The instructions about strong, intimate relationships don't come at the beginning of Paul's letter. He spends plenty of time describing the fabulous message of the gospel: Through the cross, God has rescued us, adopted us, and equipped us. And now in our daily walk with him, he directs us and empowers us. When our hearts grasp even a taste of this grace, we're overwhelmed with relief, gratitude, and the desire to honor him. Some of the biggest tests of our faith occur in these three arenas of relationships.

Too often, fear clouds and distorts our relationships. When we feel out of control, we manage people instead of loving them. We defend ourselves instead of forgiving, and we hide behind insincerity and outright lies instead of being authentic. In effect, we make deals with our spouses, kids, and co-workers: I'll treat you nicely if you treat me with respect. When the contract breaks down, we feel even more insecure and try to control more than ever. In *Relationships*, Les and Leslie Parrott comment on the paramount importance of our human connections: "We need camaraderie, affection, love. These are not options in life, or sentimental trimmings; they are part of our species' survival kit. We *need* to belong."[25]

---

25   Les and Leslie Parrott, *Relationships* (Zondervan: Grand Rapids, 1998), p. 11.

In difficult, strained relationships, different people react in very different ways—and quite often, they're married to each other! Some go into hyper-control mode: demanding, smothering, hovering, and commanding. Others control people's access to them by being distant—emotionally, physically, and even sexually. Some use harsh words to intimidate; others use silence to punish those who have disappointed them. None of these responses produce trust, love, or respect. Some of us equate control with love, but the two are poles apart. Those who smother people with attention communicate, "I don't trust you to make your own decisions. I'm controlling you because you can't make it without me." Genuine love isn't manipulative, and it isn't distant. Some have been burned too badly or too often, so they build walls to keep people out. Their goal in life is to avoid being hurt again.

Authentic love always involves risk, but refusing to love is an even bigger risk. In his book, , C. S. Lewis describes what happens when we value self-protection over love:

> To love at all is to be vulnerable. Love anything, and your heart will certainly be wrung and possibly broken. If you want to make sure of keeping it intact, you must give your heart to no one, not even to an animal. Wrap it carefully round with hobbies and little luxuries; avoid all entanglements; lock it up safe in the casket or coffin of your selfishness. But in that casket—safe, dark, motionless, airless—it will change. It will not be broken; it will become unbreakable, impenetrable, irredeemable. The alternative to tragedy, or at least to the risk of tragedy, is damnation. The only place outside Heaven where you can be perfectly safe from all the dangers and perturbations of love is Hell.[26]

---

26   C. S. Lewis, *The Four Loves* (Houghton Mifflin Harcourt, 1991), 121.

Into this cauldron of insecurity and control, Jesus steps in with unconditional love, forgiveness, and acceptance. He doesn't gloss over our flaws and sins. He looks them squarely in the eye and forgives them. His love doesn't depend on our performance; it's in spite of our attempts to impress him. How secure are we in his love? At the end of a long discourse in Romans on the certainty of God's grace and the absolute security of our adoption as his beloved children, Paul concludes with a flourish. He says there is nothing in all creation—inside us or outside us, things we've done or things done to us—that can ever separate us from God's amazing love. He explained, "For I am sure that neither death nor life, nor angels nor rulers, nor things present nor things to come, nor powers, nor height nor depth, nor anything else in all creation, will be able to separate us from the love of God in Christ Jesus our Lord" (Romans 8:38-39).

God doesn't expect us to manufacture love for others. Our capacity and motivation to love people—especially when they're hard to love—is only possible if God's love fills our hearts and overflows into their lives. We can then imitate God and love, forgive, and accept others the way he loves, forgives, and accepts us. We don't demand perfection, but we don't gloss over sin. We live in grace and truth in every relationship.

Why don't we live and love this way? There are many reasons. As we have seen, some of us are afraid of being vulnerable, so we control people or hide from them. Some of us doubt that God will work deeply in our hearts to give us the security we need so we can move toward people who are difficult to love, so we keep our distance. Some live by feelings instead of faith, letting anger, fear, and hurt dominate our lives and crowd out God's presence and promises. And some of us have divided loyalties. Our hearts are full—but of the wrong things. We care more about power, pleasure, possessions, and popularity than the riches of Christ's truth and love.

Idealizing a spouse, children, parents, or work inevitably leads to resentment and the compulsion to control them for our own good. It's human nature to manage people around us, but God has given us everything we need to genuinely love them. The passage about our most important relationships comes directly after Paul describes the power of the Holy Spirit to give us wisdom and strength to do God's will. The results of a life of dependence on God are joy, gratitude, and mutual submission. Without these, we have no hope of having meaningful connections based on the love of God. The bridge from the work of the Spirit to these relationships is verse 21: "submitting to one another out of reverence for Christ." The quality of every relationship is based on this principle—not power, money, sexual favors, appearance, brilliance, or any other external trait. The first step for spouses, children, parents, employees, and employers is to grasp the grace of God so we act like Christ in humble submission. If he was willing to step out of heaven to die for us, we can step out of our selfishness to understand and value each other.

WIVES AND HUSBANDS

People at the altar on their wedding day often have unrealistic dreams of marriage. They expect their bride or groom to fill their lives with unfettered joy, meaning, and fantastic sex. Too often, they put their highest hopes in that person—a flawed, sinful human being—and they become deeply disappointed. When we make a spouse (or child or career) into an idol, that person simply can't fill the hole only God can fill.

To wives, Paul wrote, "Wives, submit to your own husbands, as to the Lord. For the husband is the head of the wife even as Christ is the head of the church, his body, and is himself its Savior. Now as the church submits to Christ, so also wives should submit in everything to their husbands" (5:22-24). The secret ingredient in this recipe for a healthy marriage is for both the husband and wife to submit "as to the Lord." Frankly, I've found that people simply don't want to submit—to God or to each other. Until we get the primary issue of submission to Christ right, we'll struggle in all our relationships.

In Paul's day, only slaves were humble and submissive. Free men exercised power. In these male-dominated households, women and children were considered little more than property. Husbands used or tolerated their spouses and kids, but there was little affection. Into this culture, Paul's directives were revolutionary! They still are today.

A generation ago, one of the most common problems in Christian marriages was the husband "lording it over" his wife. Some men ruled their homes like a king commanding his subjects. His wishes were law, and he listened to no appeal. Some pastors taught that the husband was "the head" (which implied complete control) and the wife was "the feet" (which signified servitude). In these homes, Paul's directive to wives was severed from his instruction in the previous verse for mutual submission.

Today, perhaps after 50 years of the feminist movement, we have the opposite problem: Many men have abdicated their God-given role as the leader of their homes. Many are absent emotionally, if not physically. Divorce, unemployment, discouragement, and other factors have eroded the authority of men in our culture. When husbands and fathers are depicted in movies, it's often as bumbling, incompetent fools. This image isn't helpful for those who are trying to lead with love and dignity!

In this vacuum of manhood, many women see no option but to take control of the marriage, the children, and the family finances. Out of frustration, they assume roles that they weren't meant to have. I'm not condemning passive husbands or power-grabbing wives, but I'm pointing out that this isn't God's design. Husbands and wives are to be mutually submissive, but on the rare occasions when they can't come to a mutual decision, the husband is the decider. That's what it means to be "the head." Paul compares the husband's role as the head of the wife to Christ's headship of the church.

> Husbands, love your wives, as Christ loved the church and gave himself up for her, that he might sanctify her, having cleansed her by the washing of water with the word, so that he might present the church to himself in splendor, without spot or wrinkle or any such thing, that she might be holy and without blemish. In the same way husbands should love their wives as their own bodies. He who loves his wife loves himself. For no one ever hated his own flesh, but nourishes and cherishes it, just as Christ does the church, because we are members of his body. "Therefore a man shall leave his father and mother and hold fast to his wife, and the two shall become one flesh." This mystery is profound, and I am saying that it refers to Christ and the church. However, let each one of you love his wife as himself, and let the wife see that she respects her husband (5:25-33).

Did Christ intimidate us into submission? Did he use guilt or shame to make us obey him? Does he treat us as tools or objects? Does he see us as a necessary inconvenience? No, he loves us so much that he emptied himself and sacrificed his life for us. That's the measure of Jesus' love, and husbands are to emulate this devotion and sacrifice in their relationships with their wives. How would it affect marriages if husbands acted this way? Wives wouldn't be nearly as defensive or demanding. Just as our hearts melt when we experience God's grace, a wife's heart is filled with wonder, love, and gratitude when she feels safe in her husband's unconditional affection. Then, submission isn't nearly as big of a problem—for either of them.

In his appeal to husbands, Paul refers, too, to reason. Since a husband and wife become "one flesh," it's absurd to think of a man harming himself. A healthy man gives proper attention to his physical needs. He is aware of every pain, gives attention to every desire and need, resolves difficulties, and provides pleasures. An unhealthy person eats, sleeps, and drinks too much or too little. He doesn't care for his own needs, even when the detrimental effects become painfully obvious. In the same way, some husbands are very unhealthy in their relationships with their spouses. Paul explains that it's enlightened self interest for a man to care for his wife in the same way he cares for his own body. Just as God doesn't want anything to interfere with our relationship with him, Paul instructs the husband to avoid letting any other relationship (specifically, their parents) to come between him and his wife.

Being "one flesh" is more than sex. It means a husband and wife form a unique identity. They learn to think each other's thoughts, anticipate each other's needs, feel each other's emotions, and share common desires and purposes. A great, creative sex life is both the product of this kind of secure, intimate relationship, and it reinforces the relationship in a bond of vulnerability, passion, and delight.

Paul ends this poetic and profound section of his letter with a practical insight into the differences between men and women. Both sexes value love and respect, but the hearts of women thrive on love, and the brains of men are wired to run on respect. A description of Emerson Eggerichs' insightful and powerful book, , includes this observation: "Psychological studies affirm it, and the Bible has been saying it for ages. Cracking the communication code between husband and wife involves understanding one thing: that unconditional respect is as powerful for him as unconditional love is for her. It's the secret to marriage that every couple seeks, and yet few couples ever find."[27]

I've found this distinction to be true in my relationship with Elaine. I love her unlike I love anyone else, and I'm more vulnerable to her than anyone on earth. Others can put me down, and I can deal with it, but when she shows disrespect, it hurts terribly. We've been married a long time, and we're still learning what it means for me to love her and for her to respect me. We've come a long way—usually through the process of resolving disagreements—but we still have a long way to go. At least now we have a common language so we understand each other. That makes a big difference.

To respond appropriately to the Lord and to our spouse, we need to understand the family culture of our childhood. The way our parents related to each other and to us is imprinted on our brains like a chick thinking the first thing it sees is its mother. If our father was authoritarian and our mother compliant, we assume that's the way it should be—until we get married to someone from a very different background. Then, expectations collide and sparks fly! Sadly, mutual submission is rare in a marriage. My parents had a wonderful relationship. My father was the undisputed head of our home, but I don't believe my mother ever felt unduly oppressed. She was convinced that my dad loved her with all his heart, and she had the highest respect for him. When Elaine and I got married, I assumed I was walking down the aisle with someone just like my mother. It took a while for me to realize the culture of Elaine' family was very different from mine—not better and not worse, just different. We needed a few years to adjust to each other's expectations, and we're still working at it!

---

27   Emerson Eggerichs, *Love & Respect* (Thomas Nelson: Nashville, 2004), front flap.

The world is always focused on authority and power, or escape and protection. The kind of marriage Paul describes—one based on security, love, and humility—is otherworldly, strange, and often misunderstood, but it's an accurate reflection of God's love for us. Until Paul's letter, people looked back at Genesis for instruction about marriage, but it was incomplete. Paul adds the missing pieces to the puzzle. Mutual submission in the presence of Christ is the "mystery" revealed by Paul. From the beginning, God meant marriage to be a tangible, daily expression of his grace for the church. When this happens, disputes are resolved, people seek to understand instead of defend, they are willing to give instead of demanding their own way, and the world sees Christ's love in action. This transformation doesn't happen by osmosis or magic. It takes intentional effort to admit our selfishness, bathe our hearts in the grace of God, put off demands or escape, let the word of God renew our minds, and by the power of the Spirit, put on love and respect. When this happens in the lives of two people in a marriage, it's a beautiful, creative, life-giving, and life-sustaining process.

CHILDREN AND PARENTS

The old adage says that children need "roots and wings" to become healthy, loving, wise, competent adults. Parenting has always been a challenging task, but never more so than today. There are more distractions and pressures today than ever. Kids feel intense competition to be the best, to win a scholarship, and prove themselves. And parents feel enormous pressure to make their children succeed . . . for the child's future and for the parents' reputation. Into this pressure cooker, Paul gives brief but profound instructions to help them "put on" Christ. To kids, Paul wrote,

Children, obey your parents in the Lord, for this is right. "Honor your father and mother" (this is the first commandment with a promise), "that it may go well with you and that you may live long in the land" (6:1-3).

Martin Luther said that God hasn't called parents to raise children according to their own standards, but to raise them "in the Lord." In the same way, children are to obey their parents "in the Lord." The connection to Christ is the key element in each of these pairs of relationships. Here, Paul applies it to kids and parents. He began with the bridge verse for all Christians to submit to one another "out of reverence for Christ." How does a child show this reverence? By fulfilling the commandment etched on Moses' tablet of stone: "Honor your father and mother." Children are to love, respect, and obey their parents *because* they love, respect, and obey God. God, Moses, and Paul understood that sometimes kids feel their obedience is difficult and worthless. To combat discouragement, God gave them the promise that heartfelt obedience to their parents would result in their experience of the abundant life. The original promise focused on the land of Israel, but today, the promise is about a life of blessings now that will be fully realized later in the new heaven and new earth. Strengthened with this assurance, children are to "honor [their parents], serve and obey them, love and cherish them."[28] The promise in Exodus and in Ephesians is more about the quality of life than its length. Have you ever been around a family filled with tension and bickering? These people would trade decades of their strife-filled lives for a few pleasant and loving ones.

---

28 Martin Luther's Catechism, cited in *It's a Matter of Life and Faith: Volume 3* by David M. Albertin (CSS Publishing, 1997), p. 34.

Paul addresses the second half of this dual instruction to fathers, but both parents are included in the promise to children. In the Roman Empire, fathers were the undisputed kings of their households and absolute rulers over their children. He wrote, "Fathers, do not provoke your children to anger, but bring them up in the discipline and instruction of the Lord" (6:4). Paul's instructions apply to both parents today.

What do parents do that provoke their kids to anger? The list can seem endless, including demands, harsh criticism, comparison with siblings or other kids, inattention, distractions, and trying to win loyalty with money or gifts. Paul begins with a negative admonition to parents: Don't make your kids mad! Then he directs them to instill all the principles and practices of this letter (and all the Scriptures) into their lives so they learn Christ and walk with him in grace, wisdom, and strength. We don't just *discipline* our kids—we also *disciple* them. That's the parents' primary task.

Parents don't have to be perfect, but they need to earn trust, build the relationship, and launch their kids into maturity. Two of the most important traits of good parenting are honesty and consistency. When my children were growing up, they needed to hear me admit when I was wrong—which was often. And they needed me to be consistent from day to day, to strive to be the same man in private that I was in public. That's the way trust is built. Actually, it's the *only* way trust is built.

Developmental psychologists tell us that the parents' role changes as the child grows up. As the child enters and walks through adolescence, wise parents give increasing responsibility to the child for decisions, along with consequences. For parents, this takes as much art as science, blended with plenty of prayer and advice from parents who have walked that road before. To train kids, parents need to administer law and gospel, judgment and grace, consequences and forgiveness.

Parents make one of two mistakes in their relationships with their kids, and quite often, each parent makes a different mistake: One is too involved, but the other too distant; one is smothering, but the other provides no guidance or attention. It's easy to see where this goes. I'll use the stereotypes, which are sometimes reversed: When a detached father sees the effects of the smothering mother on a son or daughter, he backs away even more . . . which infuriates her and compels her to "make up for" her husband's inattention to the kids. This cycle continues for years, but often is punctuated with periodic promises of change, fierce explosions of anger, and simmering resentment. If the parents never notice the destructive pattern and change it, the children grow up with this model of control and avoidance imprinted on their minds and hearts. And they inflict the same pathology and pain on the next generation.

Children and parents have a tough job relating to each other. Without the compelling love of Christ, they're left to controlling each other instead of building relationships of love and loyalty. When both are in the process of growing in grace, they seek understanding, find resolution, focus on the positives, and become each other's biggest cheerleaders.

EMPLOYEES AND EMPLOYERS

Paul addresses the next couplet to "bondservants and masters," or some translations of the Bible say "slaves and masters." We need to understand that slavery in the Roman world was very different from 18th and 19th century slavery in America. Some people have wondered why Paul didn't fiercely condemn the practice. The reason is that it wasn't nearly as bad as we presume. In most cases, "slaves" in the Roman Empire were indentured servants. They served their masters for a few years, seldom more than 15. They wore the same kind of clothes as their masters, had rights and property, and sometimes even had bondservants of their own. They sometimes indentured themselves to a master to pay off a debt. In some cases, slaves were elders in churches and presided over their masters who attended the church. The kind of slavery in the American South was much different. Blacks were kidnapped and sold into permanent, grueling conditions of servitude, with little hope of freedom. The condition addressed by Paul is much more like employees and employers, so I'll use these terms.

When Paul wrote to the employees in the church in Ephesus, he referred to the secret ingredient of faith in Christ three times. He instructed them,

> Bondservants, obey your earthly masters with fear and trem-
> bling, with a sincere heart, as you would Christ, not by the
> way of eye-service, as people-pleasers, but as bondservants of
> Christ, doing the will of God from the heart, rendering ser-
> vice with a good will as to the Lord and not to man, knowing
> that whatever good anyone does, this he will receive back from
> the Lord, whether he is a bondservant or is free (6:5-8).

Paul doesn't sugarcoat difficult working environments. Some of us have grueling jobs all the time, and a few of us suffer through work all the time. Paul, though, raises our eyes to see the relationship in a new light. Instead of despising the demands of the workplace—and hating those who make the demands—Paul tells us to obey our bosses in the same way we obey Christ, consider ourselves first to be his servants, and do our work for him. We "do the will of God" (which is our voca-tion and calling) "from the heart"—not out of fear, pride, or guilt, but motivated by loyal love for God. That perspective changes everything!

Our bosses are visible and verbal. It's entirely normal for people in difficult work situations to suck up to the boss and even betray other employees if we think stabbing them in the back will win points with our employer. Paul says, "Here's a different way. Don't work to please your boss. Look beyond him or her. Work to please Jesus Christ. Consider him to be your ultimate boss." This difficult assignment comes with a perk. Paul promises God's blessings when we honor Christ in everything we do at work. Our boss may not notice the change in our motivation, but God does. He knows, he cares, and he rewards. Ultimately, we belong to and work for the King of kings. He's our Lord, our Father, and our employer.

Paul wrote to the other half of the relationship when he wrote, "Masters, do the same to them, and stop your threatening, knowing that he who is both their Master and yours is in heaven, and that there is no partiality with him" (6:9). What does Paul mean when he says, "do the same to them"? He had instructed employees to work for Christ; now he's telling masters to lead their teams for Christ. In other words, treat every employee the way you'd treat the Lord Jesus if he worked for you. To control and motivate, some employers use threats. Paul says, "Stop it! We have a common Master. Value others the way you'd value Jesus. Replace coercion with kindness, understanding, clarity, and consistency."

Paul reminds employers there is no partiality with God. In most companies, we find a natural pecking order from the president down to the mailroom clerk. Wherever we find ourselves on the organizational chart, we tend to feel inferior to those above us and superior to those below us. We carefully craft our words to impress the vice president or departmental director, but we hardly have a second to even smile at the administrative assistant who's new on the job. Paul tells employers to remember who they are. They aren't something special because they have a title on their door, and the janitor isn't trash because he hasn't received a college degree. All human beings have inherent dignity because the God of the universe has created us. We need to stop playing the game of upward mobility and downward shame. We need to see each person through the eyes of God so we highly value everyone.

Ken Blanchard was the co-author of the best-selling *One Minute Manager*. I heard him speak at a conference years after he had a spiritual awakening. He told the crowd that if he could have written the book again, he would have added that the secret to a healthy, dynamic, productive workplace is for both bosses and employees to confess their faults to each other and forgive each other. He said it would revolutionize the business environment and transform people's lives. He's right, but it wouldn't be a novel concept. Paul gave the same advice almost two thousand years ago.

NO MORE POWER PLAYS

Love, trust, respect, honor. These traits are treasures in any relationship, but sadly, they are too rare in marriages, between parents and children, and in the workplace. Changing the status quo requires courage and tenacity. We begin by peeling off the blinders that have clouded our vision for so long. We look at things like they really are. We appreciate all the good in others, and we examine our culpability in the difficult areas of our most important relationships. We don't have to depend on our own intellect and skills to make changes. We have a much more powerful resource. The writer to the Hebrews encouraged us to be ruthlessly honest because we're completely secure in God's love. He wrote,

> Since then we have a great high priest who has passed through the heavens, Jesus, the Son of God, let us hold fast our

confession. For we do not have a high priest who is unable to sympathize with our weaknesses, but one who in every respect has been tempted as we are, yet without sin. Let us then with confidence draw near to the throne of grace, that we may receive mercy and find grace to help in time of need (Hebrews 4:14-16).

These important relationships give life or suck the life out of us. Sooner or later, strains happen, and disappointments occur. If we're not careful, we can give up on ever having meaning in them again, or we'll blindly continue to use demands, pleading, or intimidation to control people we claim to love. We need a new commitment: No more power plays; no more cowering in fear. We can bring our cherished relationships to the throne of God and ask him for grace and direction.

The process of living by God's love is sometimes painful but often rewarding. When our pastoral staff team had planning retreats, we often went toe-to-toe in arguments about virtually every aspect of our work. Sometimes, people got upset. They yelled, they cried, and they got their feelings hurt. But we never left a retreat without resolving our differences, forgiving each other, affirming each other, and extending God's grace to each other. These conversations were the messy process of making sausage in authentic connections, but it was tasty sausage.

Injecting God's grace into the most cherished relationships was radical stuff in the Roman world, and it's still radical today. We may want power, prestige, and control over others, but Jesus calls us to a different way. On the night he was betrayed, Jesus met with his disciples to give them final instructions. He talked to them about a lot of things, but one of them was the importance of changing the nature of relationships. Matthew records Jesus' words:

But Jesus called them to him and said, "You know that the rulers of the Gentiles lord it over them, and their great ones exercise authority over them. It shall not be so among you. But whoever would be great among you must be your servant, and whoever would be first among you must be your slave, even as the Son of Man came not to be served but to serve, and to give his life as a ransom for many" (Matthew 20:25-28).

The will of Christ is for us to find our security deeply rooted in the gospel of grace. When we taste, feel, sense, and see the glory of God's love and forgiveness, our hearts find their true home. Old compulsions to dominate die away in the warmth of God's affection. We love others because he first loved us. Old fears of being exposed are replaced with the certainty that God knows our worst and loves us anyway. We are God's chosen, adopted, forgiven children. As his grace fills us, it spills out into the lives of those around us. We are happy to serve others because Christ served us so completely. It's the only reasonable response to his kindness, affection, and delight.

THINK ABOUT IT...

1. Do agree or disagree that these three types of relationships "give us life or suck the life out of us"? Explain your answer.

2. How do comparison and idealization affect marriages?

3. How does Paul connect the roles of husbands and wives to Christ?

4. How would you define and describe what it means to honor your parents?

5. Does Paul's instruction to children to obey their parents have a cut off age? Under what conditions, if any, are we off the hook to obey them?

6. Describe the two extremes of parenting: smothering our kids or being distant from them. How do these behaviors affect the children? How do they affect the marriage?

7. What does it mean for parents to disciple their children?

8. How would it affect your attitude at work if you realized you work primarily for the Lord? What would change?

9. If you supervise anyone at work, how would it shape your leadership if you consider that every person in your company, up and down the organizational chart, has the same Master in heaven?

7

NO ILLUSIONS

Ephesians 6:10-24

There is no neutral ground in the universe; every square inch,

every split second is claimed by God and counterclaimed by Satan.

—C. S. Lewis

aul, a brilliant and perceptive pastor, realized all the spiritual concepts he wrote in his letter could easily overwhelm the readers.
In the first three chapters, he had pointed them to the stars as he
described the wonder and mystery of God's amazing grace. These
theological truths fill our hearts with wonder and gratitude. Then Paul
applies God's grace to the nitty-gritty of real life: relating to difficult
people, finding God's purpose for our lives, making good choices for
the right reasons, trusting in the Spirit's power and wisdom, and treating the most important people in our lives like we'd treat Jesus himself.
A normal person's reaction might be, "No way. I can't do this!" Paul
understands this response, so he ends his letter with a metaphor every
reader would instantly recognize: God has provided armor for every
believer that is similar to the weapons and protection worn by the
powerful Roman legions. To be all God wants us to be, we have to
fight—and fight well.

BE STRONG

Paul began, "Finally, be strong in the Lord and in the strength of his might" (6:10). He didn't shame us by saying, "Come on. Just suck it up! Don't be a coward." He reminded us that our strength comes from a source outside ourselves. It comes from God. Every Christian who has ever been serious about following Jesus has struggled with the challenge. We see the glorious promises of the Bible, but they won't be completely fulfilled in this lifetime. We vacillate between soaring optimism and gnawing pessimism. Paul encourages us to step off this roller coaster and have God's view of things.

Many people come to church each week (or occasionally) because they want a little help with their problems. They realize their lives aren't what they want them to be, and they hope God will push them over the hump so they can be truly happy. They have a "god in a box." They pull him off the shelf when they want him to do something for them, but otherwise, they leave him alone. Years ago, I saw a bumper sticker that said, "God is my co-pilot." That's the perspective of these people. He's their doting grandfather, their waiter, their servant to help them—but they're afraid they'll find he's a cosmic cop, a fierce judge, an abusive dad, or a distant god who really doesn't care at all. (Maybe that's why they don't come to church very often.) In his seminal book, *Your God Is Too Small*, J. B. Phillips commented, "God will inevitably appear to disappoint the man who is attempting to use Him as a convenience, a prop, or a comfort, for his own plans. God has never been known to disappoint the man who is sincerely wanting to co-operate with His own purposes."[29]

Into these misconceptions, Paul's letter loudly proclaims a very different view of God.

---

29 J. B. Phillips, *Your God Is Too Small* (Touchstone, 1997), p. 49.

- We were hopeless in our sins, but God's grace has rescued us from death and hell. His love thrills us.

- We were aimless, but God has made us junior partners in the greatest enterprise the world has ever known—transforming the world and uniting all things in heaven and earth under the lordship of Jesus Christ.

- We were powerless to change anyone, including ourselves, but God has put the Holy Spirit into our lives to provide the power, wisdom, and compassion we need to do his will.

- We planned to run our own lives as we saw fit, but we now realize Jesus is the Lord who has earned our love and loyalty.

Theologians describe God as *transcendent* and *imminent*. We need to hold both of these contrasting concepts together. God is "far above all." His power, love, grace, and purposes are beyond anything we can ever imagine. When we think we have him figured out, we're in big trouble! No matter how wonderful we imagine him to be, he's more wonderful still. He is beyond our comprehension, but he has revealed enough to prove he is worthy of our trust. Ultimately, God has made himself approachable in Jesus Christ. Because of him, he's "as close as our breath." His Spirit lives in us every moment of every day. Even in the revelation of God in Jesus Christ, we have a great mystery. How can an obscure carpenter's son living in a remote corner of the Roman Empire live and die so that he changes individuals and the entire trajectory of history? It seems absurd, but it's true. The one who knows the atoms in a star in the most distant galaxy delights in our love and weeps when we hurt. Because of his awesome power and deep compassion, we find strength to face any hardship.

It's inevitable. Difficulties come our way. Most Christian teachers categorize our struggle against three forces: the deceptive messages and enticements of the world, our sinful selfishness, and the devil's designs to get us off track. Paul has addressed all of these in his letter, but now, he focuses on the devil's plots.

"WHERE'D THAT COME FROM?"

Sometimes, we can be rolling along in our lives. Things are going well at home and at work, and we feel good about God, his purposes, and our place in his plans. Then, wham! Something hits us seemingly from out of the blue. It may be a long-simmering relational problem that had been dormant for months or years, a medical emergency, a prodigal child, a job change, a fire or tornado, or a simple misunderstanding that blows up into a crisis. It could be almost anything, and it rocks our world.

Paul identified the source of these problems: "Put on the whole armor of God, that you may be able to stand against the schemes of the devil. For we do not wrestle against flesh and blood, but against the rulers, against the authorities, against the cosmic powers over this present darkness, against the spiritual forces of evil in the heavenly places" (6:11-12). When I have a conflict with someone, I often automatically—and mistakenly—assume my struggle is directly and only with that person. Paul tells us to look again. Throughout his letter, he has mentioned the fact that we live in two worlds: seen and unseen. The unseen universe is just as real as the things we touch, smell, taste, see, and hear.

We are involved in a cosmic struggle against the forces of evil. When I was in high school (back before the earth's crust had hardened), my English teacher asked our class, "Did you know you're living in a physical world you can see with your eyes, but you're also living in a spiritual world you can't see? In the spiritual world, the powers of evil are constantly at war with the power of God." This is no fairytale; it's reality. Martin Luther once had a vision of Satan that was so real that he threw his inkwell at him! In *The Screwtape Letters*, C. S. Lewis said we often make one of two mistakes when we think of the devil: "There are two equal and opposite errors into which our race can fall about the devils. One is to disbelieve in their existence. The other is to believe, and to feel an excessive and unhealthy interest in them. They themselves are equally pleased by both errors and hail a materialist or a magician with the same delight."[30] In the unseen world, our enemy is very real and has power, but God has far more. Every spiritually attuned person has at least a faint sense of the existence of the unseen world. We sometimes say, "What possessed me to do that?" It may be a more insightful question than we imagined.

When Soviet cosmonaut Yuri Gagarin was the first man to orbit the earth, he returned with a message from the atheistic Communist government to the rest of the world. He announced that he had been into heaven, but he didn't find God there. Yuri didn't understand the concept of "the heavenly places." Many Christians don't either. Heaven isn't "somewhere out there" in the vast expanse of the sky. It's a parallel universe around us—more like string theory. When we pray, we aren't talking to a God who is ten billion miles away. Yes, he's there, but he's here, too. We live and breathe in him all day, every day. And all around us is another set of forces. These are the agents of Satan, whose purpose is to deceive us, tempt us, and accuse us. Christ stepped out of the heavenly realm to earth to pay the price none of us could pay. When he was finished, he went back to the heavenly realm and

---

30 C. S. Lewis, *The Screwtape Letters* (HarperCollins: New York, 1996), p. ix.

sat at the right hand of the Father. We are "in him" in his death, burial, and resurrection. We celebrate that mystical union—in humility and exaltation—in our baptism and Holy Communion. We don't see this other dimension, but every true believer knows it's real.

When Paul said our struggle isn't "against flesh and blood," was he serious? It sure looks like real people who betray us, ignore us, intimidate us, and manipulate us! Paul is saying that our real struggle—and our real hope—is in the parallel universe of the heavenly realms. We get a glimpse of this concept in Joseph's response to his brothers. Joseph was Jacob's eleventh son and his father's favorite, so his jealous brothers found a way to get rid of him. They planned to kill him, but instead, they sold him to a passing caravan and told their father Joseph had been eaten by wild animals. The young man became a slave in Egypt. His master's wife tried to seduce the handsome young man, but Joseph resisted her. His integrity landed him in a dungeon, where he languished for many years. Finally, the pharaoh had disturbing dreams that only Joseph could interpret. The ruler was so impressed that he made him prime minister of the land. When famine struck Egypt and the surrounding nations, Jacob and his sons ran out of food. They came to Egypt with empty stomachs and the hope of finding something to eat, but instead, they were shocked to find their brother as second in command of the most powerful nation on earth! He could have had them killed, but he tested them, forgave them, and brought them to Egypt to live. When their father died, the brothers were afraid Joseph would kill them. They begged for their lives.

> But Joseph said to them, "Do not fear, for am I in the place of God? As for you, you meant evil against me, but God meant it for good, to bring it about that many people should be kept alive, as they are today. So do not fear; I will provide for you

and your little ones." Thus he comforted them and spoke kindly to them (Genesis 50:19-21).

Joseph had caught a glimpse of the heavenly realms and God's mysterious purposes. Instead of lashing out in anger at those who had callously betrayed him, he realized God had a divine purpose for what happened. It didn't make their actions right, but it put their betrayal in perspective. They meant it for evil, but God meant it for good. With this view, Joseph forgave them and took steps to care for them. The brothers were terrified, but Joseph was kind and gracious.

If you want to know what it means to be aware of God's mysterious purposes in the heavenly realms, think of Joseph's response to his brothers.

HEAD TO TOE

The image Paul paints is not of the vast army of God arrayed against his enemies, but of an individual soldier ready for battle. His readers had passed battalions of Roman legions in the streets, and they undoubtedly had heard stories of their conquests. Children looked in amazement at the uniforms, shields, and swords. Paul informs us that we need spiritual armor. To face life's disappointments, to fight against the forces of darkness, we can't afford to stand naked and unarmed. We need to be equipped, prepared, courageous, and tenacious in battle.

Some Christians assume that they can be passive and trust God to do it all. Their motto is "Let go and let God." Certainly, there are times when we have no idea what to do, and all we can do is entrust our situations and ourselves to God's mercy. But most of the time, God wants us to be active participants in his cause. In the letter, Paul has told the Ephesians that we are God's chosen children and his partners to fulfill his purposes. We are soldiers, not couch potatoes! Sometimes, I'm awestruck by the grace of God in my life. I'm amazed at his goodness, his blessings, and the love he has showered on me. Those times are precious, and they fuel my desire to be a good soldier for Jesus Christ. They propel me to get involved in people's lives and grand projects, to reach for the stars and care for the homeless. In light of all he has written so far, Paul describes the pieces of armor:

> Therefore take up the whole armor of God, that you may be able to withstand in the evil day, and having done all, to stand firm. Stand therefore, having fastened on the belt of truth, and having put on the breastplate of righteousness, and, as shoes for your feet, having put on the readiness given by the gospel of peace. In all circumstances take up the shield of faith, with which you can extinguish all the flaming darts of the evil one; and take the helmet of salvation, and the sword of the Spirit, which is the word of God, praying at all times in the Spirit, with all prayer and supplication. To that end keep alert with all perseverance, making supplication for all the saints, and also for me, that words may be given to me in opening my mouth boldly to proclaim the mystery of the gospel, for which I am an ambassador in chains, that I may declare it boldly, as I ought to speak (6:13-20).

Three times in this part of the letter, Paul tells them to "stand" or "stand firm." In hand-to-hand combat, a Roman soldier had to fight fierce warriors intent on jabbing him with a sword or shooting him with an arrow. If he was on his feet, he had a chance to fight well. If he fell down, he was toast. Paul is being redundant for a good reason—soldiers are terribly vulnerable when they lose their footing. This concept isn't new in Paul's teaching. To the Christians in Rome, he wrote, "Therefore, since we have been justified by faith, we have peace with God through our Lord Jesus Christ. Through him we have also obtained access by faith into this grace in which we stand, and we rejoice in hope of the glory of God" (5:1-2). We stand only because of the grace of God, and in him, our hearts burst with the thrill of being loved and accepted.

Over the years as I've taught this passage, people have said, "Pastor, I've tried to remember all the parts of the armor so I can put them on in prayer, but it's hard to think of them all. Can you help me?" I can. When I think of the armor, I put it on from head to toe. (I don't think Paul would mind me listing the parts in a different order.) Let's look at them.

The helmet of salvation

A helmet covers the soldier's head and protects his ability to think. Our minds play tricks on us. We're vulnerable to the enemy's whispers that we can't do enough to earn God's love, he doesn't care about us anyway, or our situations are hopeless. Satan doesn't come to us wearing a red suit and with a wicked voice. He's often disguised "as an angel of light," and his voice sounds like ours. It's easy for us to think that the whispers of doubt, deception, temptation, and accusation come from our own heads. When we wear the helmet of salvation, we pay attention to God's word, his commands and his promises. We renew our minds by riveting our thoughts on God's truths—no matter how loudly our doubts and fears scream at us.

Salvation isn't just rescue from hell. God's saving grace has a bigger end in mind. He wants to transform us from the inside out, changing our motives, our purposes, and our desires, as well as our behavior. This kind of radical transformation doesn't happen by a few minutes of worship each week. We need to do the work of putting on the helmet of salvation so we learn to think God's thoughts, value God's purposes, and live by his directives. We have the absolute certainty that the blood of Jesus cleanses us from all sin, and His Spirit lives in us to equip and empower us to live each moment in a way that pleases God. We need to fix our minds on grand thoughts of God's kindness, power, and purposes. After all, "the mind is a terrible thing to waste." The helmet of salvation helps us make the most of it.

The breastplate of righteousness

The Bible uses the term 'heart' to identify the place of reflection and emotions. When we trust in our own efforts to win God's approval, our hearts remain exposed to Satan's accusations that we aren't measuring up. Then we're vulnerable to arrogance (when we think we're doing well) or shame (when we realize we've failed). The breastplate of righteousness covers our hearts—not our righteousness, but Christ's.

The beautiful song, "Before the Throne of God Above," contains the lyrics:

> When Satan tempts me to despair
> And tells me of the guilt within
> Upward I look and see Him there
> Who made an end to all my sin
> Because the sinless Savior died
> My sinful soul is counted free
> For God the just is satisfied
> To look on Him and pardon me
> To look on Him and pardon me[31]

---

31 "Before the Throne of God Above," Charitie Lees Smith, b. 1841.

The sinless Savior died for you and me. When the Father looks at us now, he sees Christ's blood and righteousness poured out on us. We stand, not because of our good deeds, but because Jesus paid our debt. When I know I've sinned, I trust in Christ's sacrifice and righteousness. When I have doubts, I trust in his death to pay the price I could never pay. His righteousness is my only hope and protection.

The shield of faith

A Roman soldier carried a leather-covered shield to protect him in battle. If the enemy used flaming arrows, the soldiers often wet the leather to extinguish the fire. A shield could be turned to face any attacks. In the same way, our faith needs to be mobile and pointed toward the enemy's thrusts. Our faith is reinforced by the spiritual disciplines of prayer, Bible reading, confession, fellowship, service, and communion. In his *Large Catechism*, Luther wrote, "If you could see how many knives, darts and arrows are every moment aimed at you, you would be glad to come to the Sacrament as often as possible."[32] His point is that we're always in a battle. We aren't only *sometimes* in the thick of things. Every moment of every day, the forces of light and darkness are in combat for our souls. We need to strengthen and use our faith to protect us from the "flaming arrows" of the enemy's lies.

The belt of truth

God has given us his word to lead us into truth—about himself, his purposes, and our relationship to him. The Scriptures were written over several centuries by many different authors in varied cultures, but the stories and teachings form a marvelously interwoven fabric of truth. The God of the universe loves us so much that he has pierced the

---

32 Martin Luther, *The Large Catechism* (Republished by Forgotten Books, 2007), p. 124.

veil between the seen and unseen worlds to make himself known. The Bible may seem complicated and out of touch with current culture, but its insights into human nature and the complexities of relationships are clearer and more relevant than those of the most skilled philosopher or psychologist.

The truth, though, has come to us in a different way—in human form. John introduced his gospel with a revolutionary insight:

> In the beginning was the Word, and the Word was with God, and the Word was God. He was in the beginning with God. All things were made through him, and without him was not any thing made that was made. In him was life, and the life was the light of men. The light shines in the darkness, and the darkness has not overcome it. . . . And the Word became flesh and dwelt among us, and we have seen his glory, glory as of the only Son from the Father, full of grace and truth (John 1:1-5, 14).

The truth about God is found in the pages of Scripture and the life of Jesus Christ. It doesn't help, though, to leave the book on the shelf and ignore prayer as a means to connect with Jesus. No relationship is static; it either grows from attention or declines from neglect. We have at our fingertips the most important truths the world has ever known—it's truly good news!

In Luther's famous hymn, "A Mighty Fortress Is Our God," he reminded us,

> Though devils all the world should fill,
> All eager to devour us.
> We tremble not, we fear no ill,

They shall not overpower us.
This world's prince may still
Scowl fierce as he will,
He can harm us none,
He's judged; the deed is done;
One little word can fell him.[33]

The "one little word" isn't our word—it's God's word. When we trust in our own wisdom, we're in big trouble. When we use Scripture in our fight against doubts, temptations, and fear, the devil has no chance.

The Roman soldier didn't wear his belt as a fashion statement. It kept his tunic in place, held his sword's scabbard, and provided storage for other things he needed to fight well. In the same way, the truth of God holds our lives together and provides everything we need in our combat as God's allies.

The sword of the Spirit

The writer to the Hebrews informed us,

For the word of God is living and active, sharper than any two-edged sword, piercing to the division of soul and of spirit, of joints and of marrow, and discerning the thoughts and intentions of the heart. And no creature is hidden from his sight, but all are naked and exposed to the eyes of him to whom we must give account (Hebrews 4:12-13).

This is good news and bad news because God's word exposes gospel and law, life and death, light and darkness. When we reflect on the

---

33   Martin Luther, "A Mighty Fortress Is Our God," Composite Translation from the Pennsylvania Lutheran *Church Book* of 1868, *Lutheran Hymnal*, 1941.

Scriptures, God uses it to penetrate the deepest recesses of our hearts. There we find hidden, repulsive sin we never wanted to admit, but the Bible also loudly proclaims God's unconditional love and forgiveness. Nothing is beyond God's grace!

Luther once said that if we don't frequently feel the need to come to the Lord's Table for the Communion, we should read the Ten Commandments and realize how much we desperately need God's grace. If that doesn't work, we need to reach inside our shirts to feel our chests to see if our hearts are beating. If we don't sense our need for God's cleansing grace, we may not be alive!

The shoes of peace

Roman soldiers wore hobnail sandals that were much like golf shoes. The spikes dug into the ground to provide firm footing in the chaos of battle. What provides firm footing for Christians? God's perfect peace. This sense of inner strength and stability is the direct result of grasping the gospel. We don't have to wonder if we've done enough. God has done it all. The Father chose us to be his beloved children before the foundation of the world. The Son gave his life for us and forgave us. The Spirit has entered our lives as a down payment of the incredible riches of grace that will be showered on us in the new heaven and new earth. When we feel overwhelmed, when we feel like giving up, we need to remember that we can experience God's peace when we focus on the glory and blessing of the gospel. Because of Christ—and only because of Christ—we can stand strong in the middle of life's difficulties.

No matter what challenges and struggles we face, Jesus promises us his peace. He told the disciples, "These things I have spoken to you while I am still with you. But the Helper, the Holy Spirit, whom the Father will send in my name, he will teach you all things and bring to your remembrance all that I have said to you. Peace I leave with you; my peace I give to you. Not as the world gives do I give to you. Let not your hearts be troubled, neither let them be afraid" (John 14:25-27).

Communicating with the Commander

Prayer is two-way communication. We praise God for his greatness and grace, we ask him to intervene in the lives of those we love and in our circumstances, and we listen to him as he speaks to us through his word and his Spirit's whisper. When we try to pray, we can easily drift off to think about our next appointment, the show we watched on television last night, or what's in the refrigerator. We can be distracted by almost anything. Paul encourages us to "keep alert with all perseverance" because it's so easy to drift.

We are to pray "in the Spirit." The role of the Holy Spirit is to shine a light on Jesus. He helps us focus on the sacrifice of Christ, and he renews our motivation to obey him out of love instead of guilt. When we're weak and we don't know how to pray, the Holy Spirit "intercedes for the saints according to the will of God" (Romans 8:27). Many times in my life, I've faced situations that were so perplexing that I didn't even know what to ask for in prayer. When my father was near death and suffering terribly, I wanted God to go ahead and take him home to heaven, but I didn't want to ask God to take his life. So I prayed, "Holy Spirit, I don't know how to pray, so I put my Dad in your hands. You know the Father's will. May his will be done."

The apostle tells them to pray for "all the saints." We're not in this battle alone. We have each other's backs in prayer. We support each other in many different ways, but I know someone really cares when I discover he or she is praying for me. It means the world to me. I suspect I'm not the only one who finds supportive, loving prayer to be meaningful.

Paul specifically asks the Ephesians to pray for him as he "proclaims the mystery of the gospel." It seems odd that he would ask them to pray that God would make him bold. After all, Paul was a tiger in taking the gospel to the world! But he realized everything, even his strengths, came from the hand of God. Not everyone is an apostle, and not everyone is an evangelist to unreached people groups, but all of us can pray that God will open doors and open the eyes of the blind so they can see the glory of Christ and believe in him.

Paul had told the Ephesians to "put on the whole armor of God." A Roman soldier wouldn't go into combat half-dressed. He made sure he had carefully placed every piece of armor so he would be ready. In the same way, we need every element of our spiritual armor so we can fight well. We don't need to be rigid and legalistic about this, but it helps to be thorough. A friend told me that before her family takes a trip, they sit in the car and put on each piece of armor from head to toe, reminding each other of the reality of the unseen world and God's provisions for them in the struggle against evil and darkness. Many of us would benefit from this exercise. That's why Paul included it at the end of his letter. These elements of armor aren't optional for a committed Christian who is waging war against his own sinful desires, the power forces of advertising and peer pressure in the world, and the hidden but demonic forces around us.

BOOKENDS

Paul was seldom (if ever) alone in his travels. He always had a few faithful people around him. One of these was a man named Tychicus. The letter to the Ephesians (which was probably circulated to several other churches) was entrusted to the hands of this faithful friend. Paul had covered a lot of ground in the letter, but he knew that real relationships are meant to be rich and deep. The people who had loved him and learned from him for three years would want to know much more about how he was doing, how he was feeling, and his perspectives about many different issues. He assured them that Tychicus would be his personal envoy. He explained, "So that you also may know how I am and what I am doing, Tychicus the beloved brother and faithful minister in the Lord will tell you everything. I have sent him to you for this very purpose, that you may know how we are, and that he may encourage your hearts" (6:21-22).

Paul had begun his letter by greeting them with grace and peace. At the end, the other bookend is his prayer for them to experience peace and grace. He wrote, "Peace be to the brothers, and love with faith, from God the Father and the Lord Jesus Christ. Grace be with all who love our Lord Jesus Christ with love incorruptible" (6:23-24). Peace, grace, and love. Isn't that what our hearts long for? Isn't that what gives us meaning and forges strong bonds in good times and bad?

As you and your small group have studied Paul's letter together, I hope you have developed the kind of trust and love Paul enjoyed with the people of Ephesus. When we dive into God's truth and expose our hearts to one another, amazing things happen. We discover we're not alone, and our faith may be nourished and stimulated like never before. I hope that's happened to you as you've discovered (or redis-covered) the staggering love God has for you in Jesus Christ.

THINK ABOUT IT...

1. What does it mean to treat God like a "god in a box"? How does this view affect our love for God and our obedience to him?

2. What are some reasons it's important to grasp God's transcendence *and* imminence, his awesome majesty *and* his tender love?

3. How aware are most Christians of the unseen world? What are the dangers of being clueless about this reality? What are the dangers of being obsessed with it?

4. As you think through the armor, why is it important to put on the "whole armor" instead of focusing on just a few pieces?

5. Which parts of the armor are you wearing well? Which ones need some attention? Explain your answers.

6. What are some reasons prayer is crucial to our combat against the unseen enemy?

7. What is the most important lesson (or two) you've gotten from the study of Paul's letter? How will you make this lesson a habit in your life?

ABOUT THE AUTHOR

Congregations have frequently sought Rev. John Kieschnick's counsel regarding planning, management, leadership, and stewardship. Now, as a stewardship consultant and pastor coach, Rev. Kieschnick delivers on-site consulting and mentoring services to LCMS congregations and their pastors, helping them open doors to spiritual, stewardship, and leadership growth.

Prior to joining Capital Funding Services, Rev. Kieschnick served as senior pastor of Gloria Dei Lutheran Church, Houston Texas, from 1974 to 2007. During that time, he shepherded the church from 400 to more than 3,300 baptized members, ranking it the fifth-largest LCMS congregation in the country. Under his pastorate, Gloria Dei conducted seven building and capital stewardship campaigns.

Born in Walburg, Texas, the second youngest of nine children, John received a B.S. in Education from Concordia Teachers' College (now Concordia University Chicago), River Forest, Illinois. After serving two years as teacher/principal/youth director at Calvary Lutheran Church and Day School in Havertown, Pennsylvania, John entered Concordia Theological Seminary, Springfield, Illinois (now in

Fort Wayne, Indiana). He received his B.D. from the seminary in May 1970, and his M.Div. in May 1985.

Throughout his ministry, John has served on a variety of synodical boards and committees, both national and district (Texas). He has authored numerous stewardship Bible studies and programs, many of which became models for national efforts. He authored a "Christian Money Management Program" as well as *The Best Is Yet to Come: 7 Doors of Spiritual Growth*. John also helped found the Samaritan Counseling Center in Houston and served as a founding member of the Pastoral Leadership Institute Board of Directors. He previously served on the Board of Regents of Concordia Theological Seminary, Fort Wayne, his alma mater, from 2004 to 2010.

John married Elaine Trimble on July 4, 1970. Their marriage has been blessed with three children. In his free time, John enjoys "dreaming dreams" and "seeing visions," and he "plays at" golf.

USING *STAGGERING LOVE* IN GROUPS AND CLASSES

This book is designed for individual study, small groups, and classes. The best way to absorb and apply these principles is for each person to individually study and answer the questions at the end of each chapter and then spend time discussing them in a class or a group environment.

Each chapter's questions are designed to promote reflection, application, and discussion. Order enough copies of the book for everyone to have a copy. For couples, encourage both to have their own book so they can record their individual reflections.

A recommended schedule for a small group or class might be:

WEEK 1

Introduce the material. As a group leader, tell your story, share your hopes for the group, and provide books for each person. Encourage people to read the assigned chapter each week and answer the questions.

WEEKS 2-8

Each week, introduce the topic for the week and share a story of how God has used the principles in your life. In small groups, lead people through a discussion of the questions at the end of the chapter. In classes, teach the principles in each chapter, use personal illustrations, and invite discussion.

PERSONALIZE EACH LESSON

Don't feel pressured to cover every question in your group discussions. Pick out three or four that had the biggest impact on you and focus on those, or ask people in the group to share their responses to the questions that meant the most to them that week.

Make sure you personalize the principles and applications. At least once in each group meeting, add your own story to illustrate a particular point.

Make the Scriptures come alive. Far too often, we read the Bible like it's a phone book, with little or no emotion. Paint a vivid picture for people. Focus on application so people will understand how the truths from the Bible make a difference in their lives.

FOCUS ON APPLICATION

The questions at the end of each chapter and your encouragement to group members to be authentic will help your group take big steps to apply the principles they're learning. Share how you are applying the principles in particular chapters each week and encourage them to take steps of growth, too.

THREE TYPES OF QUESTIONS

If you have led groups for a few years, you already understand the importance of using open questions to stimulate discussion. Three types of questions are and . Many of the questions at the end of each lesson are open questions.

Limiting questions focus on an obvious answer, such as, "What does Jesus call himself in John 10:11?" These don't stimulate reflection or discussion. If you want to use questions like this, follow them with thought-provoking open questions.

Leading questions require the listener to guess what the leader has in mind, such as, "Why did Jesus use the metaphor of a shepherd in John 10?" (He was probably alluding to a passage in Ezekiel, but many people don't know that.) The teacher who asks a leading question has a definite answer in mind. Instead of asking this kind of question, you should just teach the point and perhaps ask an open question about the point you have made.

Open questions usually don't have right or wrong answers. They stimulate thinking, and they are far less threatening because the person answering doesn't risk ridicule for being wrong. These questions often begin with "Why do you think . . . ?" or "What are some reasons that . . . ?" or "How would you have felt in that situation?"

PREPARATION

As you prepare to teach this material in a group or class, consider these steps:

1. Carefully and thoughtfully read the book. Make notes, highlight key sections, quotes, or stories, and complete the reflection section at the end of each chapter. This will familiarize you with the entire scope of the content.

2. As you prepare for each week's class or group, read the corresponding chapter again and make additional notes.

3. Tailor the amount of content to the time allotted. You won't have time to cover all the questions, so pick the ones that are most pertinent.

4. Add your own stories to personalize the message and add impact.

5. Before and during your preparation, ask God to give you wisdom, clarity, and power. Trust him to use your group to change people's lives.

6. Most people will get far more out of the group if they read the chapter and complete the reflection each week. Order books before the group or class begins or after the first week.

TO ORDER MORE COPIES

For information about ordering *Staggering Love*
or *The Best Is Yet to Come*, go to www.gdlc.org and click on "resources."

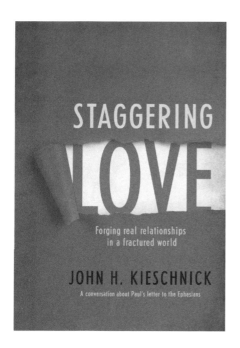

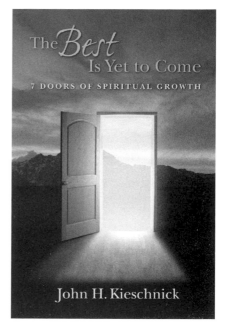